What Would You Do?

Bryant Smith

ISBN: 978-1-60594-180-6 (PB)
978-1-60594-181-3 (HC)
978-1-60594-182-0 (Ebook)

Printed in the United States of America by Llumina Press

Library of Congress Control Number: 2008908456

I would like to dedicate this book to the two people who paid the highest price, my grandparents Archie and Elvia Risper.

I am 19 years old

What Would You Do?

Greetings. My name is Bryant Smith, and this book is about an incident that took place in my family in 1969. These are the facts, as I know them. I am sure there are different opinions and ideas, but this is my account, as accurate as I can make it. There may be some facts I don't know or have forgotten over the years, but one fact is undisputable. Two people did die! I will do my best to explain why such a tragedy took place.

This is my version of what happened and how it affected me. I hope that after you read this book, you will not make the same mistakes I made in my youth. Maybe this book will set the record straight. It is as close as it gets to the true story of who did what to whom and why.

Welcome to my hell on Earth!

Chapter 1

Sweet Youth of Innocence

It was Christmas in the early 60s. I couldn't think of anyone happier then me. For Christmas, my two brothers and I got bicycles. I could not wait to get out there and try mine. Pop and Mom thought the conditions were too bad, as it had rained and snowed a couple of days earlier, but we were eager and willing to give it a try.

It can get noisy when you have seven sisters and brothers; sometimes you can't hear yourself think! That was okay; we enjoyed seeing the looks on our younger sisters and brothers' faces when they opened their gifts. We had to have breakfast first, but then the fun would begin. With any large family, you can count on disagreements followed by crying and screaming, but in the next twenty seconds, everyone was happy again. It was amazing how easily we went from one extreme to another. After breakfast, I bugged my parents until they let me take my bicycle out. At dark, the fireworks started. We had every kind of firecracker you could think of. We always lit up the sky.

Our friends from the house next door, James and Wilbur, came over to see our bicycles. However, my parents again said we should not take them out because it was muddy, cold, and icy. It looked bad outside, but I didn't care! I bugged them until they got tired of looking at my face. After about an hour, they were ready to get rid of us. Finally, Mom said, "Go do whatever you want. Just leave me alone." Those words were music to my ears. As soon as I got outside, though, I fell on my butt! That was okay. It was my first try, and I wasn't going to let one little slip discourage me. My second attempt wasn't much better. Maybe my parents knew what they were talking about, after all. By now, my friends were laughing at me, so I asked James, "Do you think you can do any better?" I let him try, and of course, he did a lot better than me. Now I felt like an idiot, as James could ride my bicycle better than I could. Wilbur took his turn riding, and he did okay, too. Thank God, I finally got the hang of it. I was ready to push it to the limits, but I had friends over, so I couldn't go too far. We took turns riding my bicycle that day, and it was a lot of fun, even with all the ice and mud on the ground, but it was only a matter of time before something happened.

I stayed near home, but my brothers were long gone. I didn't feel too bad riding in snow and ice, as it was new to me. I had hoped they would stay in the area so they could give me some pointers on what to do when I hit the icy spots, but they rode off and left me. About an hour later, my friend Randy came over. He was laughing so hard he could barely speak.

"Why are you laughing?" I asked.

"Your brothers have had an accident."

"What kind of accident?"

"Jason's chain slipped off, and he was trying to fix it when your other brother, David, came bearing down on him. David yelled, 'You better move!' Jason yelled back, 'You better not hit my bicycle!' Then, boom! David knocked his front tire off completely. Jason got mad, picked up David's bicycle, and threw it in the ditch. Then they started fighting!"

I knew something like this was bound to happen. It was only a matter of time. Two bicycles down and one to go! All and all, though, it had been a pretty good day.

My brothers managed to put their bicycles back together. I could always count on them to provide a little entertainment. In just under five hours, we'd had one broadside, one bent rim, and one twisted handlebar, and this was only the first day. Mom was worried about us falling on the ice and hurting ourselves. That was the least of our problems. We had been outside for approximately five hours and had almost destroyed all three bicycles—two in a collision and the other from constantly falling down. Thank God, it was getting dark, or the bicycles wouldn't have survived. Afterwards, even my brothers laughed at themselves.

This year was turning out to be the best Christmas ever. I liked Christmas, not just because of the gifts, but because everybody seemed so happy. Everybody tried to put his or her best foot forward. Usually, if you passed someone on the street, you just looked the other way, especially if he or she were white! At this time of year, everyone was full of smiles—blacks and whites alike. I wished it could be like that all the time. I think most of us show our true feelings during the holiday season; it gives us a chance to act the way we want without attracting attention. It gives me a glimpse into what could be if we worked at it.

James and Wilbur went home and told their parents they wanted bicycles, and in a couple of days, they had them! Man, what a good time we were going to have. The only thing left to do was to go for a ride and show off. We decided to ride around Henderson. Every house we passed, at least one person came out to ride with us, and within a few hours, we had a caravan. What a fun ride that was.

The next weekend, we went on a ride on the levee. It started off innocently enough—about twelve of us riding as fast as we could. You can imagine what happened next. The rider in front fell, and we all crashed into one another, making the little accident my brothers had seem like a quiet ride on a Saturday evening. Thank God no one was hurt other than a few bruises and our pride! After we stopped laughing at one another, we decided to go home before we killed ourselves. Thank God my brothers weren't there, or they would have laughed at us the way we laughed at them on Christmas Day. We laughed at ourselves all the way home.

"Do your brothers compete with one another?" Wilbur asked me, out of the blue.

"You don't know the half of it," I said. "They compete in everything—who has the best-looking girlfriend, who can throw the farthest, who is the strongest, who can dress the best—just about everything you can think of. Don't you and James?"

"Yeah, but your brothers are professionals! Once, we were playing a game of marbles, and I lost, of course. I wanted to play again, but he didn't want to, so I bugged him until he got angry with me, which led to a fight. During the fight, James' overalls fell off. Although I lose every time we get into an argument, I can say, 'Maybe so, but I have never had my pants whipped off me.' That usually puts an end to the argument."

"That's the best you can do? You are amateurs. Listen to this. One evening, my brothers had a dispute over the lights. David wanted to go to bed, but Jason wasn't ready. There are two light switches in our bedroom. David turned the lights off; Jason turned them back on. I knew I was in for something special! David turned them off. They were standing at different switches, turning the lights off and on. Jason decided to run to David's light switch to stop him from turning the light off again. David guessed his move and headed towards Jason's light switch. They met somewhere in the middle of the room with a few choice words. The results were the same. I lay in bed, laughing so hard my stomach hurt. If I'd had a box of popcorn and a Pepsi, it would have been like going to the movies. I put the covers over my head and went to sleep; that is the only time in my life I can remember going to sleep laughing."

After my story, we were laughing so hard we rode into the ditch!

Although my brothers were very competitive, they really loved one another. If David or I got into trouble, you could be sure Jason would be there. If one of us was about to get into a fight, Jason would do the fighting if we let him. I learned early, if I had a problem don't tell Jason. He meant well, but he never learned the art of negotiation. He was the kind of brother you wanted at your side in a fight.

They got the best of me one day when we went to pick up pecans. The rule was that when we found a tree with lots of pecans, we would pick them up together. We would all start at the same time; that way, no one would have an advantage. After looking around, we found a tree full of pecans. Jason and Wilbur started climbing. I wanted to climb also, but I was afraid of heights. My job was to stay on the ground and direct them to the limb with the most pecans. Their job was to stomp on the limbs to make the pecans fall. Either they would finish or I would tell them we had enough on the ground and they would climb back down. No one was supposed to start picking up pecans until everybody was on the ground and ready. For some reason, on this day, David started before Jason was on the ground. Well, that led to a big argument, which led to a fight. It got ugly, so I had to do something. I told them if they would stop fighting, I would give them half of my pecans. That was the only thing that stopped them from fighting. After I gave them my pecans, they seemed relaxed, too relaxed, if *you* ask me; it almost seemed planned. I felt like I had been fooled, but it was the only thing I could think of at the time. Usually, after a fight, they were angry at one another, but today they were smiling. I fell for it hook, line, and sinker!

When we got home, Mom looked at how many pecans Jason and David had and said, "That's good." When she got to me, she said, "What happened, son?"

I said, "I ate most of mine."

She just looked at me and said, "That's okay, son; *you* will do better next time."

I couldn't tell her what had happened. In my heart, I knew they got me, but there would be another day.

During the summer, we often went swimming to cool off. One little pond was fenced off, so of course we decided to take a look. It had a KEEP OUT sign on the fence, which only made us more curious. It almost seemed like an invitation. We stripped down to our shorts and jumped in. It was nice and cool, just what the doctor ordered on a very hot, humid day.

We had been swimming for about fifteen minutes when Peter said, "What is that?"

It looked like some branches sticking up from a tree at first glance. We didn't think much about it at the time and kept on swimming.

Peter then said, "Those are some funny looking branches."

We weren't too concerned about that, as it was time to prove our ability to swim by diving to the bottom of the pond and getting a handful of dirt to prove we had made it.

Wilbur said, "What the Sam Hill is that?"

We all stopped and looked back, and Jesse said, "It looks like it is moving towards us."

Peter said, "It's just branches floating with the current."

I said, "I don't think so. The current is moving in the other direction."

Randy said, "What is that?"

Wilber said, "It looks like eyes!"

We all stopped to get a better look. I started wondering what could possibly have eyes sticking out of the water. Just like in a cartoon, all of us slowly turned and looked at one another.

Jesse said, "Alligator!" I don't know who won the gold medal in the hundred-meter freestyle in the 1968 Olympics, but he would not have stood a chance against us that day. Prior to that day, I did not think it possible to swim without touching the water. Louisiana would have been proud on that summer's day because the fastest swimmers in the world were not from West Germany, East Germany, any European country, or even California. The fastest swimmers in the world were in a pond in East Carroll Parish! I had not realized I could swim so fast. Although we were only about two hundred feet from the bank, it seemed to take an eternity to reach it. Although we were in mortal danger, we didn't act like little girls; we conducted ourselves like the young men we were. We will just forget about all the screaming and yelling, "God help us," and a few other choice words that I won't repeat! After we got out of the water, we looked around to see that everybody had made it out safe. The next few minutes were spent trying to get our wind back. Then we started laughing at one another, especially at the one who called on the Lord to help him. I think we all called on the Lord in our own way, but the one that screamed it so everybody could hear him was just asking for it, and he was teased and laughed at even more. The sign should have read, "Alligator Farm," not "Keep Out."

It had been a hell of a day. I got home an hour later, tired and hungry. I went to the kitchen, where Mom was just finishing supper and heard Pop drive up. All of us kids ran out to greet him. All you could hear was "Hi, Daddy." All attention went to him. Someday, I would be the man of the house, just as Pop was.

Mom and Pop were a typical Southern family. The man earned the living, and the wife raised the children and kept the family running smoothly. Sometimes I wondered how they got together. They were so different. Mom was the practical joker, whereas Pop was mostly serious. Mom was a big believer in God, and Pop was just the opposite. Mom didn't make us go to church every Sunday, but she insisted we go to Sunday school.

My grandparents on my mother's side were also strong believers in God, so I guess Pop was fighting an uphill battle. Grandpa would preach you a sermon if you gave him half a chance. Grandpa believed in God, but he would curse in a heartbeat. He cracked me up. I think Pop felt a little left out, living in a house of Christians and being the only non-believer. Although I hadn't accepted Christ as my personal savior, I believed it was only a matter of time before I did. While we were working in the fields one day, the subject of Christianity came up.

Pop said, "I know your mother and her parents believe in God, but I don't think it makes a difference, and I am going to tell you why. We are farmers, just like a lot of other people around here. If it rains, it will rain on our property, just as it rains on the preacher's property. It is not going to skip around and rain just on the believer's property."

What Pop said made sense to me. Then my brain started working overtime. Did that mean I didn't have to go to Sunday school? This conversation was getting better and better. Somehow, I didn't think Mom was going to go along with this. Maybe it was best to keep this conversation to myself for now.

The next day, we were working in the fields again, and I was tired of chopping cotton. I wanted to play baseball with my friends. I was also trying to come up with how to tell Mom about my new way of thinking. It was getting cloudy and windy; maybe it would rain and I wouldn't have to chop any more cotton. That would suit me just fine! Oh, boy, I could see the rain coming. I was getting happier by the minute. The rain got closer and closer. With all the prayers I was sending up, it was only a matter of time. The rain got to the edge of our property and stopped! I was angry, but more surprised at what happened. Three hundred yards away was a major rainstorm, and on our property, it was bone dry! I had seen some strange things in my day, but this was ridiculous. I turned and looked at Pop, and he was looking at me. We didn't say a word to each another, but we were both thinking about the conversation that we'd had the day before. Even Pop was perplexed. I heard him say, "What the hell!"

I am not saying God sent the rain to convince me, but I changed my mind right then and there. I decided that Pop was wrong this time. I wanted to be just like Pop, except I would be a Christian! I should have joined the church right away, but I delayed acknowledging Christ.

In the fall, I was picking cotton in our field, and it was very tall and had many green leaves, which made it difficult to see your feet. Out of nowhere, I heard a voice in my head say, "If you were to get bitten by a snake and die, you would be lost!" It scared me. I could barely do my work because I was too busy looking for snakes. When we had revival at my church that year, I joined. I can't say I noticed a significant change in my life right away, but it made working in the fields a lot easier.

Early in March, we started getting the land ready for planting. Pop had a job at the sawmill in Sondheimer, so that meant I was doing most of the work on our farm. I went to work early one morning and saw two men doing something on our property. When I got closer, I realized that they were surveyors. One was an elderly gentleman, about forty; his assistant was closer to my age—in his late teens or early twenties. The assistant's job was to raise the rope when I passed so I wouldn't run over it.

I stopped for lunch about noon, and the assistant stopped also. The older gentleman had left earlier, leaving his assistant to hold the rope as I passed. I found a nice, comfortable tree with lots of shade under which to relax. I guess the assistant didn't want to eat alone, so he came over. He introduced himself, and I asked if he had brought a lunch. He said no, so I offered him part of mine. Just my luck, I had run out of cigarettes, so he offered me one of his. Before I knew it, we were talking as if we had known one another all our lives. We talked about college and our plans for the future, but our main topics were girls and firearms. He told me about his conquests, and I told him about mine. Of course, we stretched the truth a little, especially me, because at the time I had no conquests. It did make for good conversation. I was amazed to hear he was having the same problems I was. His parents were a little overbearing, but we had plans come hell or high water! It all seemed so common, but it wasn't. The assistant was white. I know that doesn't seem like much, but in the 60s, it wasn't that common, at least not for me. I think that was the first time I had an honest-to-goodness conversation with someone that wasn't black! I was amazed to find out that he had as many problems as I did. Although our parents had cautioned us against being careless, we were determined to have fun, no matter the cost!

April 14 was right around the corner, my eighteenth birthday. I was a little older now and hopefully, a little wiser. Being eighteen would open up a new world for me. I would be officially a man, the first milestone of 1969. The Tuesday after my eighteenth birthday, I rushed down to the Selective Services office to register for the draft. I knew that meant I could be drafted, but I didn't care! Secretly, I hoped to be drafted. The idea of going to Vietnam didn't bother me at all.

Next, I needed to graduate from G.W. Griffith High. That was the second milestone of 1969. I was excited about my prospects for the future. I saw only good things coming my way. Recruits from various colleges came to my high school, looking for students. Apparently, the tests I took in March had gotten their attention. I was told I had a scholarship to a college in Georgia and all I had to do was take the entrance exam and pay two hundred dollars. I went home that day, explained everything to Pop, and he said he could not afford it. As always, Pop had the last word, so that was the end of that.

A couple of days later, I saw one of the other students that the recruiter was talking to, and he said the recruiters were looking for me for the final interview. I told him it didn't matter because Pop didn't have the money. One opportunity down the drain! I hoped it didn't become a pattern.

On May 25, 1969, I became a high school graduate. I was happy and sad at the same time, as I knew I would be saying goodbye to friends and family. I thought I was prepared, but it was a lot more emotional than I expected.

Over the summer, I got my classification from the armed services. I was classified as a "1A," That was as good as it got. I asked some of my friends if they had been classified, and most of them said yes. It was a difficult time. Most of them were scared they might have to go to Vietnam. It didn't bother me that much. I felt that if I had to go to Vietnam, I would be okay. Some guys did their best to stay out of the army. Some got married, some became ministers, and the others swallowed iodine, rumored to cause spots on your lungs, which would render you unfit for serving in the armed forces. Some of the younger guys started teasing Peter and me, saying we wouldn't make it back. They said the vibrations of the guns would kill me. I was slim, but I was sure I could handle anything that came my way. I looked forward to going into the service. It would be an opportunity to travel around the world, even if it meant a stopover in Vietnam.

I told Wilbur I was thinking about volunteering. Mom overheard me, and when Wilbur left, she asked, "Are you serious about volunteering?"

"I was thinking about it," I said.

"I understand you want to serve your country, but are you sure you want to do this? You get sick to your stomach at the sight of blood. What are you going to do when you see your friends shot? It is not like what you see on television. It's not neat and clean. War is dirty and horrifying." She continued after a pause. "I am not telling you what to do; I am only asking you to think about this before you act. If you are drafted, that is one thing, but to volunteer to go and kill another human being—well, that is a lot different from what you think."

"Okay, I will think about it before acting. The main reason I was thinking about volunteering is because you get to choose the branch of the service you join."

I could see it in her eyes—she was afraid I would be hurt if I went to Vietnam. I suspect most mothers felt the same way. We had heard many horrible stories about what was happening over there.

Chapter 2

Plans for the Future

Now that I was out of high school, I had to find something to do. My friends told me about a company looking for workers in New Orleans. Peter and I decided to go, even though we didn't know what the job was. It was the first time we would be leaving home, and it seemed like a great opportunity.

I told Wilbur I would be leaving in about a week.

"I don't think you will," he said. "You could never leave your mother. You will stay here forever." He had a good laugh.

"Just wait and see."

True to my word, in two weeks, we were off to New Orleans. When we got there, we talked to someone associated with the agency that had hired us. He gave us the do's and don'ts of the company, which amounted to doing your job and not fighting on the job. Just about everything else was wide open. It was fun getting away from home for the first time.

We were taken to a place that looked like a barracks with bunk beds. As soon as we walked through the door, I heard someone say, "Damn, am I glad to see you guys." It was one of our friends from Lake Providence. It was good to see a familiar face. We laughed and talked most of the night. One of the other guys asked us to be quiet, as he was trying to get some sleep. We kept our voices down for about two minutes. The other fellow was upset, but finally he said, "Tomorrow, when you are planting that sugar cane, I will see how funny you are then."

We decided to turn in for the night. It was that or drive our roommate nuts. I got as comfortable as I could and tried to sleep. Just before falling asleep, a train sped by and, man, was it noisy. It scared the hell out of me until I realized what it was. My roommate said, "Get used to it; it happens several times a night." The next day when I got up, I had bumps all over my legs, possibly from scratching most of the night. I wasn't sure what they were from.

I asked Peter if he had been bitten during the night.

Peter said, "Yes."

This was not going to be as exciting as I thought. By the end of the day, I was very tired. After taking a shower and having supper, some of the guys wanted to go out. Peter and I decided to stay at the barracks. I was tired. The only good thing about the first day was that two of our roommates didn't get along. We had to get between them on several occasions to keep them from fighting. We mostly laughed because they were so small, we didn't think they could do any harm to one another. One of them had a strange voice. It sounded funny. We told them they had to take it easy because if the foreman caught them fighting, they would be fired. They decided to wait until the weekend to settle their differences.

That night, Peter asked if I liked working for this company. I told him no.

"Me, neither," he said. "Maybe we should leave."

The next day at noon, we quit. The foreman was a little upset, but I didn't care. Between the train and the bugs, it was time to go. Our friend tried to get us to stay until the weekend, but we had made up our minds.

The foreman gave each of us five dollars.

I asked, "Is this all we get?"

"Yes. According to the contract, you have to stay a minimum of two weeks; if you don't, you have to pay for the bus tickets and the advance that was given to you."

After we left, we realized we didn't have enough money to get home. Just our luck, there was a black man waiting at the docks for a ferry across the lake. We told him our sad story, and I think he felt sorry for us, so he decided to take us with him. Then he gave Peter and me a ride to Alexandria. Now we had enough money to get home. At the bus station, we could purchase tickets with a little left over. By now, we were hungry, and I needed a cigarette! Before I could get food or anything else, Peter told me he had met a girl, but she was out of money. He wanted the money I had left so he could buy her dinner. I needed the money myself, but I couldn't let my friend down. Amazing as it may seem, he was engaged to her before we got home. It had to be the fastest marriage proposal in history. I was hungry and tired, but seeing the look on my friend's face made it all worth it.

I was very happy when I saw a sign reading, "Tallulah, 20 Miles." I could almost taste Mom's cooking. We arrived in Tallulah at about ten p.m. on Wednesday. All we had to do now was find a way to get to Henderson. Luckily, I had many friends in Tallulah. I had gone to elementary school there. I saw my friend Brian R. Dawson, and he gave us a ride to Henderson.

When I knocked on the door, Mom let me in. She was a little surprised to see me. "Is something wrong?"

"No, but I am hungry," I said.

She started to heat up some food, and I told her I would eat it cold. While I stuffed myself, she laughed so hard she cried.

I asked, "Why are you laughing?"

"Being on your own is not as easy as you thought, is it?"

"It was fine; I just had a little setback."

She went back to bed, laughing all the way. The next morning, I told Mom what had happened.

She said, "I agree you shouldn't have to work under conditions like that. I am going to talk to the guy that gave you and Peter those jobs. Those were unsanitary working conditions. Those bugs could have made you sick."

"Don't worry about it, Mom. I am okay."

She asked, "Do you want to go to the doctor, just in case?"

"No, I think they were just mosquitoes. Don't worry, Mom. If I start to feel bad, I will go see the doctor, okay?"

"I am going to go see Peter's mother, and then we are going to go see that man."

A couple of days later, Mom told me that the guy had said he didn't know about the working conditions. He said it explained why no one stayed very long and that he wouldn't represent them anymore, but first, he was going to go see them and give them a piece of his mind.

I said, "Mom, don't worry; it is all over now."

After she got over her anger, she started laughing again. "My little man left home for the first time and almost starved himself to death."

For months after that experience, every time Peter's mom and my mom met, they would say, "New Orleans," and start laughing all over again. I learned one thing from that little trip—be better prepared the next time I left home.

Several days later, I went to Tallulah, hoping there was an opening at the sawmill. Just my luck, they did. The supervisor took me to the area where I would be working. It was possibly the hottest place on the planet. I accepted the job, but by the time I got home, I decided there was no way I was going back. I made the mistake of leaving the paperwork in my pocket showing the day I was supposed to start. When Pop saw the paperwork, he asked if I had gotten a job at the sawmill. I said yes, but that the job they'd offered me was dangerous and too hot. He just looked at me and walked away, talking to himself. I couldn't hear what he said, but I am sure it wasn't very flattering. I wasn't worried. I was sure I could find work somewhere else. To be honest, I didn't want to work in Tallulah. I don't know why I applied for a job in town. What I really wanted to do was spend my last summer with my friends. It might be the last time I saw most of them.

Growing up could be painful, but I guess that is the nature of the beast. You can't wait to become an adult, and after you are an adult, you wish you were a child again. Days spent with long-time friends sometimes turn out to be the best days of your life. I really miss my old friends.

That summer of 1969 had some disappointments, but it wasn't all bad. One evening, after a night out on the town, I came home tired and ready for sleep. It was about midnight when I got into bed, and just as I was about to doze off, I heard a noise outside. I sat up to be sure I wasn't imagining it. I didn't hear anything, so I lay back down and heard it again. It sounded like babies crying, but that didn't make any sense. It was midnight. Who would have a kid out this late at night? I lay back down and heard it again. This time, I got up and went outside to look around the front and back yards. I went back inside to bed, and as soon as I got into bed, I heard it again. This time, it was louder. I got out of bed, ran outside, and started looking in the ditches, thinking someone might be hurt, but I couldn't find anything. This time, when I got inside, I sat on the sofa waiting for the sound so I could pinpoint the location better. After about fifteen minutes, I decide to go back to bed. Early the next morning, I went outside and looked again. Maybe I missed something, but there was nothing to be found. Later that day, I was at Edward Hughes' house, telling him what had happened. His mother overheard me.

"Do you know what that means?" she asked. "It means someone close to you is going to die soon."

I wasn't sure what to say, so I tried to make a joke of it.

"I am sorry," she said, "but I am sure about this."

"Do you have any idea who the person is?"

"No, but I am sure you are going to lose a loved one."

I didn't like the sound of that at all. I played it off as if it was no big deal. On my way home, I thought about what she told me and convinced myself that she was just joking, but I didn't like her absolute certainty. Who could it be? Everybody in my family was young, including my parents. I laughed it off, and in a couple of days, I had forgotten all about it.

Two weeks later, Edward Houston had a party at his house. I was really looking forward to it. My girlfriend, Laverne, wanted to go also, so I had to ask her parents if I could take her. I was a little nervous because I had asked her parents six months earlier if it would be okay if I came to see Laverne, and her father had said no. I was shivering in my boots, but I mustered up the courage to ask her mother, and she said yes. Man, was I happy. The only thing standing in my way now was that I was afraid my heart was going to burst. I guessed things were changing for the better. Maybe they didn't hate me. As I walked towards the door, Laverne's mother called me back and said, "If something happens, you know what you have to do, don't you?" It was crystal clear. "If you get my little girl pregnant," she was saying, "you will marry her." I had to be careful or a shotgun wedding was in my future! Hell, who was I kidding? I wouldn't make it to the wedding. I would be on my best behavior tonight.

Stupid me. I forgot all that as soon as I got to the car. Laverne looked so good that evening that I could barely contain myself. Like any eighteen-year-old, I threw caution to the wind and made my pitch. It turned out to be a very good evening, and we had a great time at the party. I can't remember the last time I had that much fun. It was the perfect evening.

September was right around the corner, and I had plans to go to Los Angeles, but I needed to earn some money. I had been out of high school for four months and time was running out. I got a job at the cotton gin, and I really enjoyed working there. I was working with my friends under my cousin's supervision. I could not have had a better job. We played almost as much as we worked. When I got my first paycheck, I was surprised to see all the deductions. My friend Peter was very upset when he saw his paycheck. It was new to us, as we weren't used to having so many payroll deductions. When I got home, I showed Mom my paycheck. She said, "Welcome to adulthood!" I thought income tax was a rip-off. I had heard about it in school, but this was the first time I had experienced it. Despite the setback, I was able to save enough money to go to California. After the cotton gin closed, and I bought my ticket, it was time to head west! "Go west, young man." Isn't that what all parents tell their sons? I was eager to see the Pacific Ocean.

After I told everybody I was leaving, Mr. Eddie Carson said, "I don't believe it. You are leaving your Mommy."

I said, "Okay. In a couple of days, see if you can find me."

Wilbur said, "You know God-daddy; he just likes to play with you."

Finally, the day came for me to leave, but I wanted to see my girlfriend one last time. I went to see her around noon, and just my luck, it started raining. I tried to wait until it stopped, but it went on and on, so I had to leave in the rain. It was about three miles to my home, so I ran as fast as I could. I passed my grandparents' house, and I wanted to say goodbye, but it was late, so I changed my mind.

When I got home, Pop asked, "Where were you?"

I told him I was visiting friends.

"If you are leaving tonight, you had better hurry. Your bus leaves in two hours."

I told him if I didn't make it to the bus terminal in time, I could always leave the next day.

"If you hurry, you can still make it."

My best friend Wilbur came over to ride with us to the bus terminal. Before I left, I said goodbye to my sisters and brothers, but I could not find Mom. Finally, I gave up looking and left. I felt so empty leaving without saying goodbye to Mom. I asked Pop if I had time to say goodbye to my grandparents.

"You have less than an hour to get to the bus station," he said.

I felt like a heel for leaving without saying goodbye to my mother or grandparents. I had not used my time wisely! I convinced myself it was okay because I would be seeing them again in about a year. As I walked down the road, I looked back a couple of times. I was really leaving home. It was more difficult than I thought it would be. I was going to miss this place. The last thing Pop said before I got onto the bus was, "When you get to California, you and your brother Jason get your own place to live. You are grown men now and should not be living with other people."

I told him I would as soon as possible.

As the bus pulled out, I felt my eyes tearing up, but there was no way I was going to cry. That was for girls! Little did I know that I would be home before the year was over.

Chapter 3

CALIFORNIA, HERE I COME!

When I got to Monroe, I yelled out the window and said goodbye to my cousin who was attending college there. As we pulled out of the bus station in Monroe, the bus driver said, "Next stop, Shreveport."

I had always wanted to see that city, and now I would. It was a nice city, but it had to wait, as I was on my way to California. Finally, I got to Dallas. I really liked that city, despite the bad press associated with it. It seemed we would never get out of Texas. At ten or eleven o'clock Thursday, I saw a sign that said, "Welcome to California." I was really anxious to see all the sights. I believe it was about four-thirty p.m. when the bus driver said, "We are in Los Angeles,"

I didn't like what I saw. There were too many old buildings and homeless people in the streets. It was very depressing. I wondered if the bus driver had taken me to the wrong city because it didn't look anything like the poster I had seen, and it didn't smell that good, either.

I looked for my brother, but he was nowhere to be found. I called my aunt to let her know I was in town. She told me to catch a cab. By the time I got to my aunt's house, I was tired from the long, hard bus ride, but she was very happy to see me. About fifteen minutes later, Jason called, and we talked for a while. He told me to stay up until he got home later that night. He worked the night shift at General Motors, in the city of South Gate. After I finished talking to my brother, Aunt Betty asked if I was hungry and said, "If you want to relax, you can watch television."

I made myself comfortable on the sofa and turned on the television. It was "Thursday Night at the Movies," and the movie was *The Time Machine*, starring Cameron Mitchell. It was the best movie I had seen in a long time. As tired as I was, I had to see the ending. Soon after the movie was over, I went to bed. I could not keep my eyes open any longer. I remembered Jason coming through my bedroom. I just raised my head, looked at him, and went back to sleep. Shortly afterwards, I got up and went to his bedroom, and we talked for hours.

He said, "My girlfriend and I waited at the bus station all day for you."

"I left at night rather than in the day, so I would get here in the daytime."

"Tomorrow I will introduce you to all your relatives here in Los Angeles."

I had not realized I had that many family members out here. The next day, we also went to the Pacific Ocean. I could not believe how cold the water was. It felt as if I had just put my feet into a bucket of needles. I needed to get more familiar with the city. I had had problems sleeping because it was so damn noisy. Most nights, I heard sirens all night. I guess I had to get used to it. Where I came from, I heard howling dogs, crickets, and other life forms, but this was unbelievable.

I wanted to look for a job as soon as possible. I wasn't sure where to go, and my brother, God bless him, was not an early riser. After he left to go to work, I decided to strike out on my own to do a little exploring. I must have walked twelve blocks. I was tired and exhausted so I stopped by a liquor store for a soft drink.

As I was leaving, one the guys asked, "Do you want a drink?"

I said, "No, I don't care much for drinking."

"Okay, but this is a special occasion."

"What? Are you having a baby or getting married?" I asked.

"No, a pig was shot last night."

I thought he was joking, so I said, "That's a reason to celebrate?"

He looked at me and said, "What is your problem? Maybe you didn't understand me. I said a pig was shot."

I wasn't sure what he was talking about.

One of the other guys said, "You are not from around here, are you?"

I said, "No, I am from Louisiana."

"How long have you been in LA?"

"About five days."

He said, "A pig is a cop, a police officer. Understand?"

I said, "You are celebrating that. Stupid me."

Another said, "Hell, yes."

That is when I realized I wasn't in Kansas anymore. I moved away slowly and heard one say, "Stupid-ass country boy." They must have thought I was the biggest idiot in the city. I was never going to that liquor store again.

When my brother got home that night, I told him what had happened.

Jason said, "Most of the people in this area don't like cops. Have you noticed all the cops on the street corners?"

"Yes, I have noticed that. Why?"

"They are looking for Black Panthers. The Panthers say they are fighting so that we can have the same rights as whites."

"You mean we have the same problems out here as we do in Louisiana? That old dog and cat act?"

"There was a riot out here in Watts about five years ago, and some people have not forgotten it."

"Do you know what started the riot?" I asked.

"A cop shot a black man. At least, this is what I was told. I wasn't here, so I can only tell you what I heard."

I learned that my friend Peter lived only twenty blocks from me. I called him, and he decided to come over. I looked forward to seeing him again. When Peter arrived, we talked about the old days. I guess we were both just glad to talk to someone from home. We talked well into the night before he had to catch the bus to go home. It was one of the best evenings in Los Angeles so far. We decided to get together again soon. Somehow, Los Angeles didn't seem as empty now that one of my best friends was only an hour away by bus.

That weekend, Jason took me to a nightclub called The Apartment. It was beautiful and a lot different from the clubs from back home. After we had spent about an hour dancing, the DJ said, "We have special guest tonight." I was shocked when he said, "For your pleasure, we have Mr. Major Lance." Major Lance was one of my favorite singers.

On our way home, Jason said, "I was surprised to see you on the dance floor. When I left home, you were so shy. What happened to you?"

I said, "Well, the guys on the dance floor had a better chance of getting a girl than those holding up the wall."

"Frankly, I was surprised to hear you were leaving home so soon after high school."

"Many people thought I wouldn't be leaving home, for some reason or another," I said.

"Well, you fooled them. Me included."

The next week, while I was exploring my new surroundings, I stopped for a soft drink at the grocery store; liquor stores were off my list after my first experience. I went to a park across the street. I was sitting there resting when I heard a familiar voice. When I turned to see who it was, it looked like someone I had gone to high school with. I got a little closer, and true enough, it was. It was one of our most celebrated basketball players. I was surprised to see him, as I thought he was in college. Instead, he was here in Los Angeles, telling stories under a tree. I thought to myself, what a waste, as talented as he was. How in the Sam Hill did he end up here?

The next week, I received a letter from Mom containing a questionnaire from the State of Louisiana. I had two weeks to fill out the questionnaire and mail it back to Selective Services. I filled it out that day and mailed it back. About a month later, I received a response telling me to reregister in Los Angeles. I was hoping I had been drafted, but that wasn't my luck.

Most of the week was spent sightseeing at the museums, theaters, mountains, and all over the city. I had to find a job soon because I was running out of money.

Jason said, "You could file a claim against Louisiana for unemployment insurance. If that doesn't work, you could try the county."

I asked, "What is the county?"

"The county will give you money if you can't find a job."

"The county would give me free money?"

"Yes, if you can't find a job, you can get free money."

"How stupid do you think I am?"

He started laughing and said, "I am not kidding. The county will give you free money."

"You don't have to work for it?"

"No."

"This county is going to go broke. That is the craziest thing I have ever heard."

He said, "It is for people that have fallen onto hard times. It isn't intended to be a permanent solution to your money problems."

Now that I had been in California for a while, I was beginning to feel more relaxed. The noise didn't bother me as much any more. There were some strange customs in this state, such as free money and blacks and whites walking down the street holding hands as if it was no big deal. That would never happen in Tallulah or Lake Providence. There were many different races in this city—blacks, whites, Chinese, Japanese, Koreans, Indians—hell we had two kinds of Indians, Native Americans and Asians. It was a little funny to hear so many languages. I liked it.

My first Thanksgiving in Los Angeles was not the same as at home. Sometimes I thought if I had enough money, I might go back home. I was happy to be here and sad at the same time. There were many things to see and do, but I felt like a fish out of water. I missed the closeness of a small community, the many familiar faces you see daily. Out here, you were lucky if you saw someone from the same state. I didn't think I would miss home so much, but things were getting better.

When the telephone rang, I was sure it was one of my brother's many girlfriends, but not this time. She wanted to talk to me. I knew Jason was behind this. I thought he was trying to set me up with her. We talked for about an hour, but she wouldn't tell me her name; finally, she told me it would be a surprise. I asked what kind of surprise, and she said, "This weekend, when you and your brother go to the nightclub, I will come up and introduce myself."

I did my best to get her to change her mind, but she would not budge. I had something to look forward to, but I was a little impatient to see my first Los Angeles girlfriend. Finally, Saturday arrived. Boy was I excited. This was going to be a very special day. I bought some new clothes, and around nine p.m., I started getting ready. Jason was running late, as usual. Before he went out and played, everything had to be perfect. This night, it seemed like it took him forever to get ready.

I asked what was taking so long, and he said, "I'll be ready in a couple of minutes."

In his world, two minutes was about twenty minutes. Just before we walked out the door, my aunt came to my room, crying. She was so distraught I couldn't understand what she was saying. We asked her to repeat herself.

Aunt Betty said, "Grandma and Grandpa are dead."

Jason said, "Is this a joke?"

Aunt Betty said, "I just finished talking to Allison. My parents are dead."

I asked if I could use the phone.

"What for?" asked Aunt Betty.

"My best friend Wilbur lives next door to us. He might know something."

I called Wilbur, and he confirmed that my grandparents' house had burned down. For the next thirty minutes, I was speechless. We just sat down and mourned. I couldn't believe it. It had to be a mistake, but Wilbur had confirmed it. Then I cursed myself for looking forward to this date; it was a special date, but not anymore. Then I thought about what Edward's mother said in the summer—that someone close to me would die. The year had started with such promise, but now I saw my life slipping away!

Chapter 4

All Hell Breaks Loose

The next day, all the aunts and uncles came over to discuss when we would go back to Louisiana. Some couldn't wait and were taking the first flight out. Most of us were going to drive back. The young lady I was supposed to meet at the nightclub called the next day to ask why I didn't come. After I told her about my grandparents, she expressed her sympathy, wanted to know if there was anything she could do to help, and asked me to call her when I got back to California. That was the last conversation between us.

We arrived in Louisiana on Wednesday night. Our first stop was at Aunt Allison's house in Thomas Town. Everybody was tired, and some members wanted to stay the night at my aunt's house, but I wasn't going for that. My home was only twenty miles away. I would have walked if I'd had to. After driving almost nonstop for thirty-six hours, there was very little talking when we got to Louisiana; crying was the order of the day. After a four-hour layover, we headed for Henderson. When we got to the main road that led to my house, my heart started beating so hard I thought I was going to have a heart attack. The closer we got, the more anxious I got. Once we crossed the canal, I leaned forward to see my grandparents' home. I guess there was still a little hope this was just a nightmare, but it wasn't. Where once a beautiful white house with a green roof had stood, now there was just a pile of rubble. My home was now in sight; it was only about three hundred yards away. As soon as the car stopped, I jumped out and ran to the front door.

I knocked on the door, and after a minute, it opened. I didn't recognize the person in front of me. She looked as if she hadn't slept for days. I could see she had been crying. I wanted to ask questions right away, but now wasn't the time for that. I just said, "Hi, Mom," and gave her a hug. Then I went to the children's bedrooms and looked in on them. They looked so peaceful. I wanted to wake them up, but I didn't. I just sat on the sofa in the boys' bedroom and watched my little brothers sleep. Thank God I was home again!

At daybreak, I went outside to stretch my legs and think. I looked towards my best friend's house, and there he was, standing in the road. I guess he hadn't come over because it was too early. We met somewhere between our homes and shook hands. I was glad to see him again. I don't think we talked about what had happened. It was too soon for that. When I went back into the house, Mom was cooking breakfast. I asked if she was all right, and she said she was.

I said, "That's good. This will all be over soon." I don't usually lie to my Mom, but I couldn't think of anything else. That lie was so thin that even I didn't believe it.

My cousin asked if I wanted to walk down to my grandparents' house, but I wasn't ready for that. I was trying to avoid going to their house—or where it used to be—but I knew I would have to go eventually. What I really wanted to do was talk to Mom, but her sisters and brothers were taking up all her time. I decided to wait until she was more relaxed. I was worried that she might have a nervous breakdown. Around ten a.m., I got up the nerve to go down to my grandparents' house. Man, I felt guilty. I spent my last day here with my girlfriend, and I didn't even say goodbye!

One good thing about my return home was the welcome I got from my dog, Bull Face. He was so happy he could barely contain himself. When he saw me come out that morning, he jumped on me and ran around the house. I played with him for a while. I don't know who was happiest—Bull Face or me. I meet up with Wilbur later that day. For the first ten minutes or so, we just made small talk, but there was only one thing on our minds. Finally, I asked, "Wilbur, what happened?"

Wilbur said, "Man, I don't know. When we saw the house, it was already too late. I would have done anything to save your grandparents."

"Do you have any idea who was involved in this?"

"No, man. I have no idea."

"Did you see any unfamiliar faces in the last couple of weeks? How did no one see anything?"

Wilbur said, "Remember, it was a rainy, cold night. Most people were indoors."

"Is it possible the Klan was involved?"

"I don't think so. We haven't had any problems with the Klan, as far as I know. It was just as it was before you left. We haven't had any problems with white people."

During our discussion, we walked up to the site, trying to make sense of what had happened. It seemed so out of place here on Henderson. We hadn't had a crime for as long as I had lived here. While we looked at the scene, one of my friends from down the street came to express his profound sorrow. I asked, "Could it have been an accident?" No one had any idea. After discussing it for more than an hour, we didn't know more than we knew before. I said goodbye and headed home.

When I got home, I sat down in the boys' room to think. It just didn't make sense. Even those I thought of as being bad guys or bullies were incapable of doing something like this. It had to have been someone, but whom? Maybe we were getting carried away. Maybe it was an accident. I would feel a lot better if so.

Wilbur had said, "The day after the fire, many people came out to the site and took souvenirs."

That only made it more difficult for the police to do their job. If there had been evidence, you could be sure it was long gone. I wanted to talk to Mom, but her siblings took up most of her time. I was sure she was tired of talking about it, but I had to talk to her before I went back to California.

I had to go see Laverne. It was good to see her. Although I had been gone for three weeks, she was still my girlfriend. When I got to her house, she was glad to see me, too. She and her family expressed their regrets for my loss. Laverne asked if I had any idea what had happened.

I said, "So far, we don't know if it was an accident or something more sinister."

I visited her for hours, but most of the time, we just sat silently.

Laverne asked when I would be going back to Los Angeles, and I said I would be leaving in four or five days. She nodded then promised to come see me. We talked a little, but even she knew it wasn't a time for talking. When I was ready to leave, she walked me to the door, gave me a kiss, and hugged me. "I am so sorry, honey," she said.

"Thank you, honey, but nothing can help me now."

On my way home, I thought about the fire, but nothing made sense. The idea that I wouldn't see my grandparents again weighed heavy on my heart. I still remembered the stories Grandpa told us when we were kids. I would laugh so hard sometimes my stomach hurt. My grandpa was a very funny man. I enjoyed hearing his tall tales. I don't know who enjoyed it most, me listening to him or him telling his stories. Sometimes I think he thought I wasn't playing with a full deck. I remember one weekend when my grandparents babysat all of us so that Mom and Pop could go out for the night. My grandparents had four pear trees and two peach trees in their yard. I really liked the pears.

"Grandpa," I asked one day. "Can I have a pear?"

He said, "No, son, the pears are green; they aren't ripe yet. It will be a while before they will be eatable."

That made sense to me, so I waited for about an hour. "Do you think the pears are eatable now?"

I will never forget the way he looked at me. He must have thought I was the biggest idiot in the State of Louisiana. He mumbled a few curse words then went to the pear tree and got me one. I might have been an idiot, but I got my pear!

Grandma was just the opposite of Grandpa. She never raised her voice, not even when she was angry. When they got into an argument, Grandpa would yell at the top of his voice, but Grandma would just say, "No, Archie, you can't do that." He would get louder and louder, but Grandma would stay on an even keel, and that drove Grandpa mad! They really loved one another. The only good thing about this whole mess was that they went together.

That weekend was the funeral. It was the saddest day of my life. There was a lot of crying. I worried that Mom might not hold up very well. I went to Sondheimer to pick up supplies for the dinner that we would prepare after the funeral and stopped by a little mom-and-pop store called Griffins, but when I tried to pay for the groceries, the lady said, "No, you don't have to pay today."

She was one of the owners. "I am sorry to hear about your grandparents," she said.

"Thank you for your concern," I said.

She went on to say, "You were always a good boy. I watched you grow up; you never stole anything from me or showed any disrespect towards my husband or me. You were a good kid. Wait here."

She went into the back and got two cases of soft drinks, some cold cuts, potato chips, and an assortment of other groceries. As I looked at her, I could tell she was on the brink of crying. There were tears in her eyes. Once again, I thanked her for her concern. I was not sure how to act, as I'd always thought she wasn't too concerned with black people. I wouldn't have been too surprised if the food had come from her husband. In many ways, he reminded me of my grandpa—always joking around. When I left the store, she even shook my hand. She'd always seemed so serious when I was growing up. I guess it was necessary to operate the store.

"I wish I could do more," she said as she held the door for me.

"Thank you for the groceries."

"It was my pleasure, son."

When I got to the car, I sat there for a while, thinking about what had just happened. Could I have been wrong about her all these years? It made me wonder how many other times I was wrong about people. Maybe, I was the one that was prejudiced. I had made assumptions about this lady, and I was dead wrong. Maybe she had changed. Either way, I felt like a heel!

We had the funeral on Saturday. It was one of the worst days of my life. I had a serious problem with people crying, especially my mom. Something was wrong here. I couldn't put my finger on it, but something wasn't right. Wilbur came over and asked if I wanted to go to a basketball game. I didn't feel much like going to a game, but he convinced me it would give me time to relax for a couple of hours. I told Mom, and she said she thought it was a good idea.

She said, "Go on, son; there is nothing you can do here, and a little fun might be just what you need."

Wilbur and I went to the game. By the time we got there, it was half-time. All the seats were taken except one or two near the opponent's bench. I sat down, and before I knew it, I was having a conversation with one of the girls. She had come to support her team from Tallulah.

I said, "Our team will win."

She said, "Why don't we wait and see?"

"How about a bet?"

"Like what?"

"If my team goes over a hundred points," I said, thinking fast, "you have to give me your phone number."

"That's a bet!"

Thank God, we won by over a hundred points, and I got her phone number. I was glad I had gone to the game. Everything seemed normal for a change, but reality was setting in again. It was time to go home. I had been here for a week, and I didn't know any more than I knew when I got here.

Chapter 5

Heading Back to California

I was leaving for Los Angeles tomorrow. What a heart-pulling moment that would be. I would be saying goodbye to my family twice in less than a month. We leave for Los Angeles at twelve a.m. Aunt Sally told me she would wake me up when it was time to go. At about eleven p.m., she came to my room and told me we were leaving in about an hour. I said okay, but went back to sleep. She came back and said, "Honey, it is time to leave. You have to get up."

I told her I wasn't going and went back to sleep. The next morning when I got up, Aunt Betty wanted to talk to me. She said, "Maybe it would be best if you stayed for a while longer. Why didn't you go with Sally last night?"

I said I wasn't sure.

"Maybe it is for the best. Your mother needs someone she can count on."

I thought to myself that she had Pop for that, but I had to admit things weren't adding up. I agreed to stay a little while longer. I was waiting outside for my ride when my brother Jason came up to me.

He said, "You know, some people think Pop had something to do with Grandma and Grandpa's death."

I was stunned. I couldn't believe it. I said, "Are you out of your mind?"

"I am just telling you what I heard."

"They had better not say that to me!"

I had hurt his feelings. He was only telling me what he had heard, and I was taking it out on him. He patted me on the shoulder and walked off. I regretted talking to Jason that way, but I was angry.

Aunt Betty took me home to Henderson. I could tell Mom was glad to see me.

"You changed your mind about going back to Los Angeles?" she asked.

"Aunt Betty and I thought it would be best if I stayed until this mess was over."

One of my sisters asked if I was staying, and I said, "Yes, for a while longer."

"Good!"

I think they'd missed me as much as I missed them. When I walked outside, Edward's mother happened to be driving by. She stopped and said, "I thought you went back to Los Angeles."

"There has been a change of plans."

"I am glad you changed your mind."

She was the second person glad I'd changed my mind. I didn't know if they liked having me around or if there was something else. Now that I was back, though, what was I to do now? When I got a chance, I had to let my girlfriend know that I hadn't gone back to Los Angeles, but first, I had to talk with Mom. I hadn't had time to talk to her and there would never be a better time than right now. I squared my shoulders and went back inside.

"Mom, do you have time to talk?"

She said, "Sure. What is on your mind?"

"Is everything okay?"

She said, "Yes, why do you ask?"

"People are acting strange. As if they have to censor themselves when they talk to me."

"You can't control what other people say or do. Most people are just curious about what happened."

I said, "You are probably right. My imagination is running wild again."

Mom put my fears at ease, but I didn't know why I was so worried. Maybe I was overreacting.

On Friday, I went to see my girlfriend, the only bright spot in my life. Besides, I thought it best to let her know I was still home to keep other guys from moving in on me. She was surprised to see me. She said, "I thought you were gone."

"I changed my mind."

After about an hour of visiting, I had to go home. I got a nice hug and a kiss before I left; boy, I needed that. The thing I liked most about her was her sense of humor. I needed all the humor I could get. I began to feel a little better and to wonder why I was here. My grandparents' death was probably just a bad accident. I guessed the butane blew up, a fire started, and my grandparents couldn't put it out. Then why did I feel the way I did? It wasn't just me that felt this way. Aunt Betty felt it, too, or she wouldn't have asked me to stay and watch out for Mom. Were we reading something into this that was not there? Were we preconditioned to think the worst? Well, I was not going to drive myself crazy looking for something, and I was not even sure I knew what I was looking for. I decided I wasn't going to worry anymore.

By the time I got home from my girlfriend's house, I was more at ease than I had been in days. The kids were outside playing and having fun, oblivious to what was going on. I had been waiting for things to get back to normal, but I was about to have my world turned upside down again.

Pop said, "Did you know some people think I had something to do with this crap?"

I said, "What crap are you talking about?"

"It is rumored that I had something to do with Archie and Elvia's death."

"Who is saying that? They had better not say it to me. The first one that does is going to get his head knocked off."

"Calm down, son. If you get into trouble, that could make it bad for me. They will say that you are a bad seed, like me."

"I know you are not going to take this lying down."

"You can't stop people from talking. I just thought I should be the one to tell you before you heard it from someone else."

"Unbelievable!"

Just when I was beginning to feel better, this crap came up. What was going on here? "Mom, have you heard the lies accusing Pop of being involved with Grandma and Grandpa's deaths?" I asked her.

She said, "Yes, I have heard some of the rumors."

"Why didn't you tell me?"

"It wouldn't do any good."

If I could have been granted one wish just then, it would have been to wrap my fingers around the neck of the SOB spreading those lies. This had turned out to be a great day, hadn't it?

I went to my favorite place to think—underneath a tree in our back yard. First, was it possible that Pop had anything to do with this tragedy? No! Second, who would benefit from pointing the finger at him? If I could find the answer to that question, I might find the murderer. I still thought it was a tragic accident, but I now knew what my brother was trying to tell me outside Aunt Allison's home. I wished I had listened to him or waited until he told me who told him. Family members are always suspects, but this time, the gossips were wrong. I couldn't wait to tell some of those jackasses "I told you so." It was just a rumor. In two weeks or so, all this would blow over and someone else would be the suspect.

A couple of days later, my grandmother, my pop's mom, came for a visit. It was a surprise because she never came to visit. She came into the house and wanted to talk to us. "He did it. I know he did it," she said.

I couldn't believe what I was hearing. Pop's own mother believed the lies! I wished Pop could hear her. I wanted to say something, but it would come out wrong, and I didn't want to be disrespectful. After a while, I couldn't take it anymore. I just got up and left the room. As I was leaving, she said, "He did it because he did it once before."

What the hell was she talking about? He had done it before? I thought my grandmother's mind was playing tricks on her, but why would she say that if it were not true? There had to be a logical explanation, but what the hell was the answer?

The next day, I walked down the street to the Watson family home. After I got to Ronald's house, I remembered that Ronald had wanted to talk to me about something. I had been avoiding talking to him because I was tired of hearing people say how sorry they were. I just wanted to forget it and go on with my life.

As soon as we were alone, I said, "Ronald, is there something on your mind that you would like to discuss?" I could see he was a little nervous, so I said, "I know what you wanted to tell me, but it is okay. I know you loved my grandparents."

"Yes, that is true, but that is not what is on my mind."

"Okay, let's go outside and talk about it, if that is okay with you."

We walked outside, and Ronald said, "I hate to tell you this because our families are so close."

I said, "Just take your time and say what is on your mind."

"You know how I felt about Mr. Smith. He gave us jobs when no one else would."

I wasn't sure what he wanted to say, but it was causing him a lot of stress. "Okay, Ronald, just spit it out. I don't have all day while you make up your mind to tell me."

He said, "Your grandparents told my grandmother that your pop told them he needed money right away. They had a week to get it."

I was speechless. I didn't know what to say. Ronald wouldn't lie about something like that. "Have you told anybody what you told me?"

"No way!"

"Good, don't tell anyone. Keep it to yourself until we can find out what happened. If this gets out, it could cause problems for Pop."

As I walked away, Ronald said, "Bryant, why would your grandparents tell my grandmother that if it wasn't true? It was one week before the house burned down."

I did not want to believe it, either, but it didn't look good for Pop. "Ronald, do you believe my pop is guilty?"

"I don't know what to believe anymore. Do you believe your pop is guilty?"

I didn't answer him. I was in shock.

On my way home, my mind ran wild with all kinds of thoughts. One thing was for sure—Ronald's mom, Mrs. Sinclair, wouldn't say it if it wasn't true. There wasn't a nicer, kinder person on God's green earth. How could I explain this? If this was true, Pop was in a lot of trouble! I had to ask Pop about this, didn't I? What if his answer didn't make sense? What would I do then? I thought it is best to keep this to myself for the time being. I wondered if Mom knew about Pop's threats. I needed to slow down. This could be a big misunderstanding. I needed to take it easy. I was getting ahead of myself and had to wait until I had more facts. All I had now was hearsay, which didn't mean anything. I felt a little stupid, walking down the road, talking to myself. I needed time to think.

The next day, I went to visit Laverne. When I got to her house, I got the usual greeting—a big hug and a beautiful smile. I needed some time away from all the rumors going around. I was there for about an hour when Laverne's mother came in.

She said, "They are trying to blame your father for this, aren't they?"

I said, "I think they are."

"I am sorry, son. We don't think that over here."

I thanked her for her positive attitude.

Laverne said, "Someone came over a couple of days ago and told us he knew your pop was guilty."

"Who said he was guilty?"

She said, "I can't tell you because you might get angry."

"I won't get angry, but I need to know who is spreading those rumors."

Finally, she decided to tell me, and man, was I surprised when she told me who it was.

She said, "My father told him not to come over to his house accusing that boy of anything unless he had proof. He said he wouldn't have that kind of talk in his house."

"Your father defended my pop?"

"Yes, he did."

"I am surprised," I said, I'm touched.

"My daddy likes you; he just wants you to respect him."

"I didn't think he liked me."

"I told you he did."

"Then why, when I asked permission to come see you, did he say no?" I asked.

"You caught him on a bad day."

I began to feel a little better; at least I had some people on my side for a change. This was turning out to be a good day, and it came from an unlikely source. It looked like the tide was changing in Pop's favor. I went home that night with a strut in my walk; I didn't feel so alone anymore.

The next day, my older brother David and I were lying around watching television when we heard a car pull up outside. We looked out of the window and saw a police car in our driveway. We went to the front door to see what the officer wanted.

The officer said, "We would like to ask you and your brother a few questions, if you don't mind."

David said, "Why not? Come on in."

The officer said, "No, not here. We would like to talk to you at the police station in Lake Providence."

David said, "Fine, let's go."

We went to the police station, and they took us to a small interrogation room. The chief of detectives came into the room a while later, and said, "Have you talked to your father about the fire?"

We said in unison, "Yes, of course."

"What has he told you?"

David said, "Why you are asking us these questions? We don't know anything. When it happened, I was in Milwaukee and Bryant was in Los Angeles."

"We know that. We want to know if maybe you heard something. People get nervous when they talk to the police. We were wondering if someone told you something about that night."

I said, "Okay, I will tell you word for word what I was told so there are no mistakes."

"That's great. Now what did he say?"

"My pop said he parked his truck across the bridge because he didn't trust the bridge. After he parked his truck, he started walking home then remembered his truck was low on gas. He wasn't sure how low because his gas gauge was broken. He went to his neighbor's house to get some gas then walked back and put it in the truck. After that, he went home, watched a little television, and went to bed."

The chief of detectives nodded, and said, "That's exactly what he told us." He thanked us for talking to him and told my brother and me that he would have someone take us home in a few minutes. After the officers left, we waited for them to come back, but they were taking their time.

David said, "There is something fishy going on here. They think Pop is mixed up in this crap."

"Do you think Pop is guilty?" I asked.

"No, I don't think so."

"I don't think so, either. Why would Pop want to hurt Grandma and Grandpa? It doesn't make any sense." I paused then continued, "Even if I knew something, I wouldn't tell these people."

"It doesn't matter; we don't know anything."

"That is for sure. I think they are barking up the wrong tree."

After about thirty minutes or so, they took us home. When we got home, Pop was waiting. "What did the police want?" he asked.

"They wanted to ask David and me a few questions," I said.

"Like what?"

"They wanted to know where you were the night of the fire."

"What did you tell the police?"

"I told them exactly what you told us," I said.

"Is that all you told them?"

I said, "Yes, I don't know anything else."

Then he asked David the same questions. Later that night, he asked us the same questions all over again. This didn't feel right; it seemed almost as if he had something to hide. By the next morning, I was tired of the third degree!

I asked David, "Did Pop talk to you again?"

He said, "He has asked me the same damn questions about five times. Have you noticed his eyes when he talks to you?"

I said, "Yes, he looks scared."

"I don't know what is wrong with him, but he is acting very strange."

I went to Mom. "Is Pop all right?"

"I think so," she said. "He is just trying to deal with this as best he can."

"Mom, I know he acts strange sometimes, but this is strange, even for him."

Mom said, "Keep this to yourself, but last night he thought he heard something outside. He got out of bed and got the gun. I tried to wrestle it from him, but I couldn't. I told him if he went outside and shot someone, I would take the kids and leave. That calmed him down a little. I told him if there were cops outside, they had guns, also. If he shot at them, they would shoot back. He calmed down a little and went back to bed." She paused. "You need to talk to David."

"About what?"

"Ask him what happened when he and Pop went to the place."

The next day I found David and asked, "What happened when you and Pop went to the place?"

"We had to go out to the place for something. I don't know why he wanted me to go with him, but I did. When we got there, he gave me some meaningless task while he went down by the canal. When he got back, I asked him what he was doing, but he didn't answer."

I said, "There isn't anything down by the canal."

"I know. That is what seemed so strange."

"Did you see him take something or bring something back?"

"No, I didn't see anything."

"You think he was doing something he had no business doing, don't you?" I asked.

"I am not sure just yet, but his behavior was very weird."

Later on that day, I asked Mom what she thought was going on down by the canal.

She said, "I don't know, but it does seem strange."

I said, "Okay, Mom. I think I will take a ride out and look around."

"Are you crazy? What if he finds out you were down there? If he does have something down there, and he sees you looking around?"

"Mom, I will be careful. I will go when he is at work."

"What if someone sees you and tells him? What excuse will you have? Stay away; it is too risky."

After listening to all the strange things that were happening, I wasn't sure what to think. It looked bad for Pop, but I was sure there was a reasonable explanation. I wasn't sure what it was, but I was sure Pop would be vindicated.

I sat under my favorite tree for hours, trying to make sense of this madness. It looked like Mom and David no longer believed in Pop's innocence. I hated to think that Pop had anything to do with Grandma and Grandpa's death. The more I thought about it, the more confused I got. There was only one thing I hadn't tried. I could ask Pop to explain his strange behavior. Maybe if we talked he would put all my suspicions to rest—but how could I approach Pop and tell him I thought he was lying? He was not the kind of man that handled criticism well.

Several days later, Mom came to me early in the morning. "I have to talk to you."

"Okay, what's on your mind?"

She said, "Let's go for a walk."

"Mom, it is cold outside. Are you sure you want to go for a walk?"

"Yes."

When we got outside, she said, "The house is full of listening devices."

"Why would anyone want to bug our house?"

"Never mind that now. We have more important things to discuss. This is going to be hard for you to accept, but you have to know. Remember that your father said he was gone for about twenty minutes the night my momma and daddy died? That is a lie. I was watching television, and a program I wanted to watch came on at six p.m. About fifteen minutes later, your father left to put gas in his truck. When he left, I was watching that program, and by the time he got back, it was almost nine p.m."

"Mom, he told the police officers he was gone for about twenty minutes."

"I know, and that is a lie; he was gone much longer. It was more like two to two and a half hours."

"Mom, do you know what you are saying? The only reason he wasn't arrested is that it was impossible for him to commit the crime in the time he was gone. If what you just told me is true, he had plenty of time to commit the crime."

"I know, and there is more I have to tell you. A couple of nights ago, David and I were in the boys' room by the heater when your father came in. He opened the top of the heater and put something like plastic in the fire. David and I didn't say anything, but we looked at one another. It was so strange. The next day, I looked in the tool shed, as it was unusual for him to spend so much time there. He was washing a raincoat, and that made no sense. Your father never washed anything in his life. It was a raincoat I had never seen before. It had stains all over it."

"What kind of stains?"

"It looked as if he had spilled something on it."

"Could it have been bloodstains?" I asked.

"Absolutely!"

"Where is the raincoat now?"

She said, "I don't know. It is no longer in the tool shed; he moved it."

"Mom, why is Pop telling so many lies?"

"You have to decide that for yourself."

"Do you think he is involved?"

"That night, your father came into the bedroom screaming that my parents' house was on fire. I looked out the window, and the flames were already over the top of the house. I got dressed, ran into the kids' room, and told them to stay in the house until I got back. I ran to my parents' house as fast as I could, screaming for Mom and Pop to get out of the house. I tried to get in the front door, but there was too much smoke and fire. I ran to the back, and it was burning also. I broke one of the windows, and black smoke rushed out. It made me dizzy. I screamed as loud as I could for Mom and Pop to get out, but I heard no response. My hand was bleeding from breaking the window. Your father told Randy to stay with me, and he went to the other side of the house. After about five minutes, he came back and said there was no way to get in. When parts of the house began to fall, I knew it was too late. Even though my head and hands hurt, I still tried to find a way to get inside. Your father said it was too late; they were probably dead. He said they were probably trapped in the pantry. I didn't think much of it at the time, but the police found their bodies in the pantry area."

"Mom, I don't know if I want to know all of this."

She said, "I know, son, but you have to know what happened."

"Did you look around to see if they had gotten out?"

"No. After about an hour, there was the scent in the air of burning flesh. In my heart, I knew they were dead."

I asked, "What was Pop doing?"

"Nothing. Most of the time, it seemed more like he was trying to keep me out of the house, not trying to help me get in. He claimed he was pulling me away because he thought the butane tank might explode. When the roof fell in, I knew I was too late to save them."

"Mom, you think he did it, don't you?"

She said, "Yes, I do! I was in denial for a long time, just like you, but eventually, you have to accept things the way they are. Bryant, what are we going to do?"

I wasn't sure how to answer. If I believed what I just heard, there was no way I could believe he wasn't involved. I walked away and thought about it for about a minute. I looked at Mom and heard myself say, "He is guilty as charged, Mom."

"I know, but what are we going to do?"

"First thing I am going to do is go next door and call the police."

Chapter 6

The Day of Doom

The walk to my next-door neighbor's house was the longest walk of my life. All the way there, I tried to think of what could explain the inconsistencies in my pop's story. I knew what I had to do, but I hated it. At my neighbor's house, I asked permission to use their telephone. I hoped the police officer wouldn't pick up the phone. It would give me a little more time before I ended my pop's freedom. The officer picked up the phone on the first ring. Just my luck.

I said, "My mom and I think my pop was involved with my grandparents' death."

The officer said, "Are you sure?"

"Yes, we are sure."

He said, "Okay, we will pick him up today after he gets off from work."

I thanked our neighbors for letting me use their phone and walked home. Wilbur was there. I told Mom what the police officer said, and she said, "Good." Then she collapsed.

Wilbur helped me get Mom up to her bedroom, where she cried for a very long time. It was the first time I had seen my Mom cry since my return. I think it had finally caught up with her. Wilbur went to the living room and started playing music on our record player. I'm not sure what the song was, but it was a sad song.

Mom said, "Please don't play that song."

I went to the living room and took the record off, then went to the front door and threw it as far as I could. Wilbur looked at me, but I was in no mood to explain. I just said, "Mom doesn't like that record; play something else."

I called my aunt in Los Angeles and told her what had happened. She said, "It is about time. How is your mom holding up?"

I said, "She is okay, considering what we have done."

"I am sorry it had to end like that, but it was the only way," she said.

"It is okay; we did what we had to do for all of our sakes."

I said good-bye and told her I would keep her up-to-date on any new developments.

Later that day, the deputy chief of police came to pay us a visit. His name was Mr. Dennis. "I'm glad you finally realized that Mr. Smith is a murderer," he said.

"I didn't believe my pop could do something like this," I said.

"People like to think a family member couldn't be involved in something so tragic. I would like to say that this is the end, but it isn't; it is just the beginning!"

Mom said, "When will he be arrested?"

"Today. You don't have to worry. He will not be coming home tonight. Who made the call?"

I said, "I did."

"What made you change your mind?"

"Mom and I had a long talk. Afterwards, there was no other choice."

Mr. Dennis said, "I am truly glad you changed your mind. Your mother was in extreme danger."

"How was she in danger?"

"We have known for a long time that your father was guilty, but we couldn't prove it. The key to solving this case was your mother. She is the only one that knows how long he was gone. If he was telling the truth, she had nothing to worry about, but if he was lying, she became a liability. What if he thought she would talk eventually? If that were the case, he had to decide if he was willing to risk his life on her word, since she was the only one that knew how long he had been gone. He could easily kill her and claim it was an accident. He could say she fell or something and we would be hard-pressed to prove otherwise. That is why we were so concerned. Now I have to ask a hard question. Mrs. Smith, how long was he gone?"

I spoke before Mom had a chance and said, "He was gone for almost three hours; at least two and a half hours, for sure."

"Is that true?" the officer asked my mom.

She said, "Yes."

"That is good. He had plenty of time to commit the crime. When we tell him we know he was gone for more than twenty minutes and can prove it, he will not have a leg to stand on." He paused then said, "May I talk to your mom in private?"

I said, "Okay," and walked away. They talked for about ten minutes then he left. When he was gone, I looked at my mother. "Mom, what did he say to you?"

She said, "He thinks you are a fine young man. You knew something was wrong so you decided not to leave, even though you didn't want to believe your father was capable of committing a crime. He also said you might have to testify in court. A spouse does not have to testify against a spouse, but you can tell what you know. Let's not talk about that now; that is a long ways away. Just know that the day might come."

We sat quietly for about an hour, watching the clock. Pop got off work at two p.m., and the closer it got, the more nervous we became. If he came down the street, I didn't know what I was going to do. There was no turning back now. By four p.m., I felt a little better because that meant he wasn't coming home. They had him! I felt sorry for Mom. She had lost not only her parents, but her husband, too. It must have been a living hell for her! I decided to call Aunt Allison and tell her what was going on.

"The police arrested Pop," I said.

"When did they do that?"

"Around two p.m. today."

"It is about time. He must have been crazy to think he could get away with murder."

When David got home, I told him Pop had been arrested.

He said, "Are you sure?"

I said, "Yes, the police called and told us they had arrested him."

I don't know why I didn't give him details. I guess I was a little ashamed of what I had done. I just didn't see any other way out. It was him or Mom, and Mom hadn't done anything wrong! Pop had left us no choice. The hardest part was the waiting. The next move was Pop's. Mom, at least, seemed a little more relaxed. She could sleep. I was getting ready to go to bed when I realized I couldn't sleep. What if he got out? I got out of bed, dressed, and sat on the sofa.

I didn't believe he would be coming home, but I couldn't take the chance. I guess I was more nervous than I thought. As I sat on the sofa, I had plenty of time to think about what had happened. I was sure I had done the right thing, but that didn't make it any easier. My God. I called the police on Pop! What a bastard I turned out to be.

I went outside to sit under my favorite tree, as I always did when I was worried. As soon as I walked out the door, Bull Face, my dog, ran up to me. I sat under my tree, thinking about everything that had happened, and started crying. I put my hands over my mouth so no one could hear. Men don't cry! Bull Face looked at me crawled over to me until he could put his head in my lap. If I didn't know better, I would think he knew I was hurting. I rubbed and patted his stomach for a while then got up and started back to the house. He followed me closely until he started running. For the next ten minutes or so, we just chased one another in the yard. For those glorious few minutes, both of us were very happy. I felt a little better, thanks to my dog. I went back into the house and prayed for the next couple of hours. I was so confused. I didn't know what to do.

After that day, I watched my brother start to drink more and more. I think he was trying to forget what was happening. I wished I knew how to help him. It didn't seem like God was doing much to help the situation. The next day, the deputy chief of police, Mr. Dennis, returned.

Mr. Dennis said, "I have good news, and I have bad news. We have Mr. Smith in custody. That is the good news. The bad news is that if he gets a good lawyer, he could get out on bail until the trial begins."

I asked, "What is Mom supposed to do if he gets out? She is afraid of him."

"I am sorry, but there is nothing we can do. The law allows bail in most cases. Just calm down. It will take a while before he can get a lawyer and arrange for bail. He may not even be able to post bail, as it will be very expensive. I understand you own property in Madison Parish?"

Mom said, "Yes, we do."

"He could use his property as collateral for bail."

Mom's face changed after Mr. Dennis left.

I said, "Mom, don't worry. David and I will be here for you."

"You don't know that man when he gets angry."

I was trying to be positive, but I knew we were in trouble. We couldn't catch a break.

Aunt Allison and Uncle Watson came to visit. We told them what Mr. Dennis had said, and Uncle Watson said, "We will try to stop him from making bail, but I am afraid it is useless." Uncle Watson looked at me and said, "Can we go for a walk?"

Aunt Allison stayed with Mom as we headed down to where my grandparents' house was.

Uncle Watson said, "When you were a child, your father and I were friends. One day, your father and I were talking about our in-laws. I said we have some tough ones, don't we? Your father said, 'If I had my way, both of them would be dead.' I thought he was just joking, so I played it off, but he was serious."

I said, "I know you are kidding!"

He said, "No, I am not. Your father said, 'That old man should be shot and his wife, too, because she goes along with him.' He hated them. I knew then that he was dangerous. After he realized I didn't feel the same way, he stopped talking. I tried to convince myself he was joking, but here we are, ten years later, and it appears he wasn't."

I didn't know what to say. "My god, Uncle Watson."

"Yes, son. Me, too."

When I went home, I waited until my aunt and uncle left then asked, "Mom, why did Pop hate Grandma and Grandpa so much?"

Mom said, "When I started dating Edwin, he came by the house, and I told him to go away. When he left, he slammed the door. You know how Daddy felt about people slamming his doors. That made him upset."

I said, "Mom, why did you tell him to go away?"

Mom said, "I had been playing with John, my little cousin, and had a headache, so I had gone to my bedroom. When I heard the knock at the door, I thought it was John, and I told him to go away. When Edwin returned, I told him what had happened, but it was too late, and the damage had already been done. Daddy confronted him and told him to never come to his house and act like that again. After Daddy and Edwin finished their talk, Edwin told me that that old man didn't know who he was messing with. That was the beginning of the hostilities. Everything was all right between them for a long time, though. Just when I thought everything was okay, Daddy asked Edwin if he could borrow his poison gun to spray his crops for bugs. Edwin said, 'Sure, just let me know when you are finished, and I will come pick it up.' About a month later, Edwin hadn't heard anything about his poison gun, so he went out to see if everything was okay. When he got to Daddy's house, he saw his poison gun was outside and had been rained on. The valves were rusted. Edwin asked Daddy why he hadn't sent word he was finished using it so he could pick it up." Daddy said he'd told two people to tell Edwin he was finished, and had assumed he was in no big hurry to come get it. Edwin said, 'Bullshit, it is *your* responsibility to get word to me; come to my home, if necessary.' One thing led to another, and before I knew it, we were in a full-fledged feud. Daddy offered to pay for damages, but Edwin was angry, and it escalated from there. It never did get any better. After we left, I tried to calm him down, but your father was so mad. He said, 'All that old man had to do was put it in the barn until I got out there to pick it up. Your old man thinks he can make a fool out of me, but I will make him pay for this someday."

"Mom, are you telling me they have been fighting over a two-hundred-dollar poison gun?"

"There were other things, but that was the major one. Over the years, Momma and I tried to patch things up between them, but they were stubborn as mules and wouldn't budge."

By the next day, I was so frustrated and mentally drained that I needed to get away for a while. I knew exactly what to do—go see my girlfriend! Although I wasn't in the best of moods, I had to escape for a while. "Mom, I am going to go see Laverne."

She said, "Okay," but she didn't look okay.

"Don't worry, Mom; I will ask David to stay here with you."

I asked David to stay home until I got back, and he agreed.

When I got to Laverne's house, I wasn't in very cheerful mood.

Laverne said, "What's wrong?"

"Nothing."

"That's not true. I know when something is bothering you."

So I told her what I had done.

Laverne said, "I know you are kidding."

"I wish I were."

"I don't think I could turn my daddy in, no matter what he did."

"Do you think this was easy for me? A couple days ago, I would have agreed with you. Under normal circumstances, I probably would have kept my big mouth shut, but these are not normal circumstances. Sometimes you just have to do what is right, regardless of whom it hurts."

"Are you sure he is guilty?"

"If he isn't, he is doing all he can to make himself look guilty. There have been too many lies. It is difficult to believe someone when he continues to lie. Some of his excuses just don't make any sense."

"Have you asked him to explain his explanations?"

"No."

"Why not?"

"I am afraid of his answers. Furthermore, he can't explain away all the inconsistencies in his story. I have to get home; Mom isn't comfortable being alone."

I said my good-byes and headed home. When I walked in the door, I saw Mom peeping around the corner of the hallway. "Oh, it's you," she said.

I said, "Yes, Mom. It's me."

"He left me."

"I don't understand. What do you mean, 'He left me'?"

"David left me here by myself."

I couldn't believe it. "I told him I wouldn't be long and to stay home until I got back."

"I know, but he told me I would be all right, and then he left."

I can't tell you how angry I was. "I'm sorry, Mom. I will not leave you here alone again."

"What if he had come home and I was here by myself?"

"That was my mistake, Mom, and it will not happen again. Don't worry the man of the house is home now."

She smiled and said, "Okay, man of the house."

That was the first time I had seen Mom smile in a long time.

As I lay in my bed, I wondered if I had done the right thing. What if we were wrong and he was innocent? I didn't know if I could live with myself if he were innocent after what I had done. In my heart, I knew he was guilty. Then why did I feel so guilty? If it were just me, I would have grounds to reconsider what happened, but Mom and David felt the same way. All three of us couldn't be wrong.

The next morning, Mom and I were talking about Pop and Grandpa's disagreements. I said, "Mom, it doesn't make sense that Pop would hold a grudge for such a long time."

Mom said, "They did learn to get along a little better over the years, but that last incident started it all over. About three years ago, your father wanted to rent Daddy's property and went over to talk to him about it. He wanted to rent the property for two hundred dollars an acre; Daddy wanted three hundred. When Daddy said no, your father got angry. He said, 'Isn't your daughter worth the extra hundred dollars?' Daddy said, 'Of course, but this is business.' When your father got home, he was furious. He said, 'That old man told me no after all I had done for him.' I said it was Daddy's property, and he had the right to ask his own price. Your father said, 'I knew you would take his side.' I tried to explain that I didn't tell Daddy what to do."

"I remember that," I said. "He was upset for a long time."

"Your father didn't understand that Daddy was willing to let him rent the land cheaper than anyone else, and he hated Momma because he thought she should have convinced Daddy to rent it at the price your father wanted. I told him that Momma didn't tell Daddy what to do, just as I didn't tell him what to do, but when your father got angry there was no talking to him, so I didn't say anything else about it."

I could see that there was something else she wanted to say but was holding back, so I asked her about it.

Mom said, "I was waiting for the right time."

"What is it, Mom?"

"I am moving."

"Moving where?"

"To our cousins in Omega."

"Why?"

"Your father will get out on bail, and when that happens, I don't intend to be here, and you can't go to our property anymore. Your father sold it."

I guess I was in shock. I just stood there. I wanted to say something, but I wasn't sure what. "How do you know he sold the property?"

"We were sent word. Any ideas you had about going out to our property to look around, forget it; it's too late now."

"Mom, did you sign any papers?"

"No."

"I don't think he can do that without your signature."

"I know. That is why I am looking for an attorney. Don't worry about that now. We have more important things to worry about. I have to be out of here in a couple of days."

I said, "Okay, Mom. The kids, David, and I will take care of the house."

"No way am I leaving the kids. They go with me! You can come if you want to."

I said, "It is best that someone be here when he gets out."

"I know. You and David take care of the house, but I have to leave."

It was hard watching Mom get ready to leave. When the day finally came that she was ready to go, I watched Mom and the kids get in car and drive away. I was sick to my stomach. It seemed like goodbye was the only thing we said to each other lately. I saw tears in Mom's eyes as she walked out of her house for the last time. I was at a loss for words. As they drove away, my brothers and sisters' little hands were sticking out of the windows, waving goodbye. I went to my favorite tree out back and cried like a baby. I always thought, no matter the problem, I could find a solution. This time, I was powerless to do anything. It was for the best, and I knew it, but I could only imagine what the kids were thinking. I was an adult, and it was terribly confusing to me; I could only imagine how confusing it was to them. I had to get myself together. As the police had said, it was only the beginning, and we had a long ways to go.

My best friend Wilbur came over; at least I had someone to talk to. David acted as if everything was all right. Maybe he was more mature, but he was handling it a lot better than me. I wanted him to be as angry as I was. The problem was I wasn't sure who to be angry with!

Later that evening, David, Wilbur, and I were just kidding around in the living room, and I heard something outside. All I could think of was to get the gun and go outside to see. I got the gun out of Mom and Pop's bedroom and went outside. I looked and looked, to no avail, then went back inside the house.

David said, "Are you crazy? What the hell are you doing?"

I couldn't answer because I didn't know. I lost it and started crying again, and I couldn't stop. Wilbur came over and said, "Man, I understand how you feel, but you have to get yourself together."

I went to the back room and stayed there until I could contain myself. I was going to pieces. The worst part was that I didn't know why this was happening. It was as if someone or something had said, "Let's screw up Bryant's life," and boy, they were doing a stupendous job. Maybe that was my punishment for being so damn arrogant. Mr. Self Assured had turned into a crying wimp.

Later that night, David left to go to Tallulah to stay with our only remaining grandmother and Wilbur went home. I was all by myself, and it was one of the most uncomfortable nights in my life. I sat quietly in the back bedroom. I had to come up with a reasonable explanation for why Mom was not home if Pop came home tonight. Simply telling him she wasn't here wouldn't be good enough. What if I told him she was at Aunt Allison's house? No, that wouldn't work. He didn't get along with Uncle Watson. That could lead to more trouble. I hoped he didn't come home until Mom found a permanent place to stay. I was thinking of a good lie if when I heard a knock at the front door. My heart started pounding so hard I thought I was about to have a heart attack. I didn't think he would come so soon. I mustered up the energy to open the front door, and to my surprise, it was Wilbur.

"What are you doing here?" I asked.

"I came to keep you company. I was a little afraid to come over here with you waving guns around, though."

"You jackass; I wouldn't shoot you."

It was a relief, but anyone but Pop would have been welcome. We sat around most of the night, laughing and talking about the good old days.

Chapter 7

Christmas Sorrow

Christmas Eve was upon us, and this was not going to be a good holiday for any of us. I spent it waiting for Pop to come home. I was sure the police were going to let him out for the holidays. I was invited to share Christmas with two families, but I turned them both down because I wasn't sure where I would be on Christmas Day. Wilbur tried to convince me to spend Christmas with them. I told him I would come over if I had the chance.

I got up early Christmas morning as I always did. I had never realized just how empty a house could be. I felt like I was in *The Twilight Zone*. There was no one there but me, so I decided to go see Mom and the kids, even if I could only stay for a little while. I had to see all of them.

Mom asked, "Do you have plans for Christmas?"

"I am going to share Christmas with Wilbur and his family."

"That's good. I would hate to think you were by yourself on Christmas Day."

"I have plans. Don't worry. I have so many invitations for Christmas I don't know who to spend it with."

"Would you like to stay out here?"

"I wish I could, Mom, but I have to go home, just in case Pop gets out of jail. If he is released, you will need to know right away. The only way that can happen is if I am home or nearby when he comes home."

"I understand, son; my little boy has grown up."

I said my goodbyes and left.

As I started walking, I didn't look back. I was afraid I would lose it. I rushed to the car and drove away. I felt it coming on. I was finding out, in the worst possible way, just how emotional I was. I had always thought I was immune to these kinds of feelings. As I drove away, I glimpsed over my left shoulder to see them one more time. I pulled to the side of the road to gather myself. They weren't as happy as they had been in the past, and there was nothing I could do to help them.

On my way home, I convinced myself they would be okay. This was only for a short time, and it would end soon. When I turned onto the road leading to our home, I saw smoke. Someone was burning something. As I got closer, I saw what had happened. The neighbor's home was on fire. Thank God, everyone got out okay. It seemed I was not the only one having a terrible Christmas. I offered my help, but it was too late. The roof was falling in by the time I got there. Those of us there just stood and watched that family's home go up in smoke. The deputy chief of police came by and asked what happened. I told him I wasn't sure. I felt sorry for them.

The deputy chief asked, "Is your mom okay?"

I said, "Considering, she is okay."

The deputy chief said, "You and your family have been through a lot this year. Don't worry. This will end soon, and you can start a new life."

"It isn't that simple."

The deputy chief said, "I know, but we have to try. Why did you change your mind about going back to California?"

"I'm not sure."

"Whatever the reason, I am glad you changed your mind. It would have been extremely hard on your mother if you hadn't. By the way, do you have your driver's license?"

"No."

The deputy chief smiled and said, "Do me a favor, and get your license."

"I will get it as soon as possible."

When I got home, I went to the kitchen and opened the cupboard to see what I had to eat. I hadn't prepared anything to eat for Christmas. If I wanted a Christmas dinner, I would have to cook it myself. I should have listened to my mom. She wanted to cook for

Christmas before she left, and I told her I was going next door. It didn't matter. I didn't feel much like eating anyway.

It was Christmas Day, and I was alone and wondering if Mom and the kids were as miserable as I was. This had always been my favorite holiday, but now I hated it! For some reason, I went and looked in the kids' bedroom, and Mom and Pop's bedroom. I don't know what I was looking for, but I had to look.

I went outside, and there was my trusted friend Bull Face. He was as happy to see me as I was to see him. I broke the rules of the house and let him inside. I sat on the sofa; he got comfortable on the floor and went to sleep. I was envious of him. I would give anything to sleep so comfortably. There was only one thing left to do tonight—pray. I prayed for hours. I got up and went back outside. I felt something on my face, and when I wiped it off, I realized that I was crying and didn't know it. I was in bad shape. I needed to get myself together. I thought about going to my favorite tree to think, but that wouldn't help this time. No matter what I did, it wouldn't change anything. I was between a rock and a hard place and powerless to do anything about it. I went back inside and sat on the sofa. I heard a knock at the door, and it was a pleasure to see Wilbur.

"What are you doing, man?" he said. "Are you sitting here by yourself? Man, you know you can't do that. It will only make things worse. Why don't you come over to our house for Christmas dinner?"

"I'm not hungry,"

"That is no excuse, and if you don't come over, I am going to stay here with you. I refuse to let you sit here by yourself on Christmas Day."

Finally, I said, "Okay, I will come over for a while."

We sat around making small talk, but my mind was on one thing. I appreciated what they did for me that day. They talked about the good old days and didn't bring up the current tragedy. I thought going over to Wilbur's home would make me feel better, but watching them open Christmas presents just reminded me of what I had lost. I was worried about Mom and the kids. At least they were safe. I knew

Mom was more comfortable, and that alone made me feel better. After about two hours, I decided to go home. I couldn't stand any-more of them trying to cheer me up.

I went back to the tomb I called home. I hadn't realized just how big the house was until I had it all to myself. My sisters and brothers were always fighting. What I wouldn't give to see that right about now! With seven sisters and brothers, sometimes you can't hear yourself think. Now all I heard was silence! I began to wonder if God really cared for me. I had done my best to be a decent person, and this was my reward? How could God let something like this happen? I prayed for most of the evening, between fits of rage and anger. Finally, I asked God to do me one favor, and if he did it for me, I would be a spokesman for him the rest of my life.

"God, when I wake up tomorrow, make everything as it was before I went to California. Make this terrible tragedy just a nightmare," I prayed as sincerely as I could.

The next morning, when I woke up, I was afraid to open my eyes. I said another silent prayer. I was facing my grandparents' house (it was about three hundred yards away), looking through the window. I said, "God, please do this one thing for me." I slowly opened my eyes, but nothing had changed. Where my grandparents' house once stood was still just an empty lot. I was so angry I started cursing, I should have known better. I had always thought prayer was supposed to change things. It didn't look like it was doing me much good. I was so angry I could scream. I felt like my faith was slipping away. Maybe some people had good reason to praise God, but I couldn't think of any right now. He had let me down! What was the point in being good? It did you no good. I was told one Christian could chase a thousand non-believers and two Christians could chase ten thousand. Most of the people in our family are Christians. We had one non-Christian, and he was chasing us all over the place. What was wrong with this picture? When all hell broke loose, you think God might come to your rescue. It didn't look like it to me. My praying days were over!

I got up and made myself some breakfast. When I sat down to eat, I didn't feel the need to bless the meal as I always had. I felt like I was in this world just to be tormented. I was angry. Life wasn't fun anymore. I worked around the house most of the day, trying to find things to do. I took a break, sat down in my bedroom on the sofa, and realized I was angry with the wrong person. God had nothing to do with this. The person responsible for all of this was Pop. I was ashamed for being angry with God. I began praying and asked for his forgiveness. All my anger turned towards Pop.

What the hell was he thinking? Did he honestly think he could get away with murder? All that stuff he had taught us for years was a lie. He used to say, "If you want something, earn the money to pay for it, and if you can't earn enough to buy it then you don't need it. Don't ask anyone to do for you what you can do for yourself." His words seem so shallow now. Not that the idea was wrong, but he expected us to live up to a standard he was unable to live up to. I would never trust anyone again. How could I have been so wrong? I knew Pop had a temper, but I couldn't have ever imagined him going this far. If he were having money problems, he should have said something. Was I blind or just naive?

The next morning when I got up, I wondered what was going to happen today. I didn't feel much like doing anything. I had begun to have terrible headaches, which I assumed were caused by stress. Before I went into public, I put on my public face. I didn't want anyone to know how bad off I was. Sometimes I felt like a walking zombie. I laughed at all the jokes, but there was nothing funny to me. I know they were just trying to cheer me up, but it was no use. I was almost as angry at myself as I was at Pop. Before I left to go to California, he had asked me to stay to home and help to raise another crop. I had refused. Could this tragedy have been avoided if I had just stayed home? I wouldn't have had time to help him another season before I was drafted, but he didn't know that. All he could see were his three older sons leaving. The more I thought about it, the more depressed I got. I must have been a big disappointment to him. I should have told him my plans before I left but I didn't. Mistake number one! Nevertheless, his solution made me want to puke. I would never forgive him.

Wilbur came by to tell me Edward was having a holiday party. He wanted to know if I wanted to go.

I said, "Sure, I don't have anything else to do."

"Good! You need to get out and take your mind off your problems for a while. A little perfume will do you a lot of good."

I went to Laverne's house to tell her about the party, and she wanted to go. She told her mother, who said, "Okay, but you'd better be careful."

I knew exactly what that meant—no sex. We left and headed to the party.

Laverne said, "I have known you for six years and dated you for two, and I have never been to your house." So we stopped by for a while.

I told her not to expect too much, as my housekeeping skills weren't nearly as good as Mom's. When we got inside, she wanted the grand tour. I showed her all the empty rooms.

Laverne said, "Your house is bigger than I thought."

We sat down in the living room and talked for a while. I really was enjoying her company when I heard a knock at the door. Of all the nights, who the hell could that be? It was Wilbur's little brother. I was puzzled as to why he came over. He had never done that before.

I asked, "Is something wrong?"

He said, "No, we saw the lights go on in your house and wanted to be sure it wasn't being burglarized. I came over because we thought you were at the party."

I said, "We will be leaving soon. I just stopped by to pick up something before we went to the party."

He laughed and said, "Okay, I will tell Momma everything is okay over here. Good night." He left with a big smile on his face.

Laverne said, "He is going to tell everybody he saw me at your house."

"Don't worry. Our families are close, and if I tell him to keep it to himself he will."

"I hope so. If my family found out I was at your house alone with you, they would not be happy."

Shortly after, we went to the party and had a wonderful time. Only then did I realize how badly I had needed to relax. As always, Laverne was exactly what I needed. She was kind, humorous, sexy, and a joy to be with. She didn't let me think about all the bad things happening. She just wanted me to have fun. I was thankful, for the evening did more to lift my spirits than anything else had. Afterward, I felt more energetic than I had in a very long time. She could be a handful sometimes, but I guess all of us were when we were eighteen.

The following day, I went by Wilbur's house to talk to him. When I walked in the door, his parents started laughing. I wasn't sure at the time what was so funny.

Mr. Carson said, "Did you have a good time last night?"

"Yes, I did. It was a nice party."

"I'm talking about before the party."

Mrs. Carson said, "You are having a good time while your parents are gone, aren't you?"

"No, Laverne and I were just talking. She wanted to see our house, and I wanted to make sure the house was locked."

Mr. Carson said, "I am sure you were the perfect gentleman." He looked at me and laughed. "Boy, do you think I am crazy? I understand. It takes an hour to check the doors. I know what you were up to." He laughed as he left the room.

I went to the back room where Wilbur was, and he was laughing.

I said, "Why are you laughing?"

"I am sorry, man, but you got busted. Don't worry. They won't say anything to her parents."

"They have nothing to say because they didn't see anything."

Wilbur looked at me and said, "It looked suspicious. What happened?"

"Shut up."

"Okay, you seem more your old self again."

"Yes. I feel better than I have in a very long time."

Wilbur laughed. "I know that's right."

"Shut up," I said, laughing with him.

After an hour or so, I left to go see Mom and the kids. Mom asked, "Are you okay?"

"Sure, Mom. I'm fine."

"I don't like you living there by yourself."

"Don't worry, Mom. I am a grown man."

"I know, but if something went wrong, you would be there by yourself with no one to help you."

"I am not in any danger. Please, don't worry."

"I will worry until this is all over. That is my right, being your mother. I do have some good news. I found a house for rent in Tallulah. We can move in soon."

"How soon?"

"In a couple of days."

I said, "Okay, Mom. That's good. Maybe you will be at ease after we all move."

"I have one other thing to do before I get too comfortable," said Mom. "I have to go back to the house."

"Why?"

"I have clothing there for me and the kids, and there are dishes, blankets, and other personal items I want to get out as soon as possible. We don't have to worry about furniture. The new place is already furnished."

I said, "I will tell David."

"Don't worry about that. He is living in Tallulah already. We will tell him when we get there. Allison told me Edwin has people watching us."

"Maybe Pop doesn't know where you are."

"They are watching the house to see who comes and goes. Sooner or later, he will find out where I am, and I would prefer not to be here when that happens. I don't want to create problems for the nice people here."

"Mom, I know things look bad for Pop, but is it possible that he is innocent?"

"Do you believe he is innocent?"

"Sometimes, Mom. I'm not sure."

"I know, son, but look at all the evidence and the fact that he has lied so many times. I don't believe him anymore. He was gone for at least two and a half hours, and he told the police he was gone for fifteen or twenty minutes. That was the first thing that got me thinking. I know you desperately want him to be innocent, but we have to accept things the way they are, not the way we want them to be."

I said, "I know, Mom, but there has to be a reason. I thought about it for a long time, and I can't think of it. Sure, he didn't like Grandpa much, but that isn't a good enough reason to commit murder."

Mom said, "About two weeks before my parents died, Diana went up to see them. While she was there, Daddy asked Diana to help count his money. Daddy was mostly blind and couldn't tell the difference between a one-dollar bill and a five-dollar bill. She told me she counted fifteen one-hundred-dollar bills alone, never mind the fifties, twenties, or fives."

"Did Pop know that?"

"He might have. I don't know for sure."

"Okay. That might be true, but we were doing all right, weren't we?"

Mom said, "We had enough money to pay our bills, but there wasn't much left over."

"That was the motive—money!"

"That is as good a reason as any."

"Do you know why he chose that night?" I asked.

"I have no idea. Maybe he would have done it another night."

"Why would you say that?"

"A week earlier, I went up to see Momma and Daddy, and as I was walking up the driveway, I saw a man standing by the hedges. I couldn't see much—just from his waist down to about his knees. I had never been so scared in my life. I knocked on the door, but it seemed like it took forever for Daddy to get to the front door. I felt a lot better when he turned on the porch light. As soon as he unlatched the screen door, I rushed in. He asked if I was okay, and I told him what I'd just seen. He told me I was seeing things, probably a shadow or something. I told him I hadn't imagined it. I knew what I'd seen. He asked why someone would be standing outside the house, and I said I didn't know. He told me to calm down and asked if I'd gotten a good look at the person. I had to admit I hadn't, but I said I'd been afraid. I told him to lock his doors and windows, and then I ran home as fast as I could. Daddy kept the porch light on until I was home.

"The next day, I went to see Momma and Daddy, just to make sure they were okay. Everything seemed fine. Daddy said, 'I told you there was nothing to worry about.' After a while, I began to think I had imagined it. Maybe Daddy was right and it was just shadows. A couple of days later, I had forgotten all about it."

"If he did rob Grandma and Grandpa," I said, "he couldn't afford to be caught with the evidence. He would have to hide it somewhere. That is what he hid on our property! He couldn't afford for anyone to find that money. He would have had a lot of explaining to do if someone found it. I am definitely going out to the place to look around, and if I find that money or any of Grandma and Grandpa's property, it'll be proof."

"Yes, it would, except the property isn't ours anymore. You will be trespassing on someone else's property. Furthermore, you can be sure if it were there, it is long gone now. There is no way he would have sold the property without retrieving his loot."

Chapter 8

A Quiet Before the Storm

Right after the New Year, we moved into our new home. It wasn't very big. It was only two bedrooms and not very spacious. The girls took one bedroom and the boys took the other bedroom. It wasn't what we were accustomed to, but at least we were together. After moving in, I told Mom I was going to look around. I went downtown and saw some friends I hadn't seen in years. We had spent six years together at Wright Elementary in Tallulah. On my way home, a car passed, and I heard someone mention my name. I thought it was one of my friends. The car stopped, and a young lady got out.

"Do you remember me?" she asked.

I recognized her. She was the young lady I met at the basketball game in Lake Providence.

"Are you visiting, or were you looking for me?"

"I just moved to Tallulah," I said.

She said, "You're kidding."

"No. I just moved in today."

"That's great. I live about three blocks from here."

We talked for a while, then I said, "I have to go home, but I would like to see you again."

When I got home, David was there and had one thing to say. "This house is too small."

Over the next few days, I met family members I didn't even know I had. My cousin Dedra wanted to show me around town and show me all the good places to go. I wanted to tell her I had been coming to Tallulah for a long time, but she was having so much fun telling me about the town that I decided to just listen. After she finished, I explained that I had gone to school at Wright Elementary.

"Really? Then you are already familiar with the town."

"Yes."

"Why didn't you say something?"

"You were having so much fun talking that I just listened," I said.

We laughed and hugged.

"Do you go to the night clubs in town?" I asked.

"No way."

"Afraid to dance?"

"No, I just don't like going to places like that. I want to get a job where I can help people. Maybe I will be a missionary and go all over the world, helping people. Does that sound strange to you?"

"No. As a matter of fact, I envy you. I know what it is like to have a dream. I hope it works out for you."

"What is your dream?"

"All my dreams are on hold for now," I said.

"I understand, but what are you going to do after this nightmare is over?"

"I plan to go back to Los Angeles and have some fun for a while. I had planned on volunteering for the armed forces."

"Have you thought of working for God?" she asked. "Maybe as a minister or a missionary?"

"I'm not right for that kind of work." The idea was appealing, but I thought I would do more harm than good.

"It's not too late to join the armed forces."

"It is too late for that, too."

"Why?"

"We will be moving to Los Angeles in three or four months, and there is no way I am going to desert my sisters and brothers, or my mom."

She looked at me and smiled, saying, "Maybe you are closer to God than you think."

We talked a while longer then Dedra and I went our separate ways. It had been a good day. I saw old friends and met new family members. Maybe it would not be so bad after all. I just hated living in the city. All my life, I had lived on our own property in the country.

Now I was living on someone else's property, and I hated it. Maybe I just missed Henderson.

The next day, Mom introduced me to our landlord. She lived in the front house, and we lived in the house in the back. After about ten seconds, I knew she was a talker. She went on and on. I don't think she even took time to breathe. She didn't give you any time to answer her questions. After about twenty minutes of nonstop verbal abuse, she laid down the rules of the house.

"No noise! No parties! None of those fast heifers coming to this house." That one was directed at me. Then she turned to Mom. "You are a handsome woman, but I don't want a lot of men coming over here."

Mom said, "I am married with five young kids. That is the last thing you have to worry about."

"I am a Christian woman," said the landlady. "Are you?"

"Yes, I believe in God," said Mom.

"That's good. How about that young buck? Your son?"

"Bryant is a good boy, and you will not have to worry about him."

"Good. I don't want any problems with you and your family. Just keep the noise down and pay your rent on time, and we will get alone just fine."

After she left, I said, "I think she is nuts."

"It will be all right after she get used to us," said Mom. "I am sure we won't have any problems with her."

There was a mom-and-pop grocery store about a hundred yards up the street from us, so I went to get a few things that we had forgotten. I made friends with a young brother that worked there. He was determined to fix me up with a girl. Sometimes I would go up there just to talk, but I just couldn't get into the conversations the way I wanted to, as I did not want to talk about our family's tragedy. There were many things that I was just not ready to discuss. Even though I was around old friends, I couldn't shed the feeling of emptiness.

That weekend, Wilbur came to Tallulah. Boy, did we have a good time. I introduce him to some of my old friends, and we had a ball partying that weekend. I hated to see Wilbur go home that Sunday, but I knew he had to get back to work.

The next week, I went to an event at Wright Elementary. I heard someone calling me, turned around, and saw Debbie, one of my sisters.

"Where are you going?" she asked.

"I am going to the ball game at Wright."

The schoolteacher came over and told Debbie not to talk to strangers.

Debbie said, "He's my brother."

Mrs. Hampton said, "Okay. I didn't know."

"Hello, Mrs. Hampton," I said. She had been my sixth-grade teacher.

"How are you, Bryant? Where have you been?"

"My parents moved from Madison Parish to East Carroll Parish."

"I had wondered what had happened to you. It is good to see you again. This is your sister, I assume?"

"Yes."

"I will take good care of her."

"I don't want her to get any special privileges," I said.

"You don't have to worry about that."

The next day when Debbie got home from school, she told me that since Mrs. Hampton knew she was my sister, she expected her to know all the answers. "Mrs. Hampton says you were smart in school."

"I don't consider myself smart," I said. "But I am all right."

"Whatever the reason, it's not doing me any good."

Chapter 9

He's Out

I was kidding around with some friends at the store when Diana ran in and said, "Pop is at the house." I ran to the house as fast as I could, and when I got inside, Pop was sitting in the living room talking to Mom. My uncle was on the front porch with his pocketknife open.

I walked in, and Pop asked, "How are you doing?" I told him everything was okay.

Mom was as nervous as a cat in a dog pound. I moved closer to give her a little support and then the police arrived. They told Pop he had to leave.

Pop said, "I am not doing anything. I just came to see my family."

"I am sorry but you have to leave," insisted the officer.

"Did I do something wrong? Is there a law against me seeing my family?"

"I am sorry, Mr. Smith, but you have to leave, or you will be arrested."

Pop got up and said, "It is a damn shame that a person can't even see his own family."

I followed him out, and Pop said, "I want to talk to you later."

I said, "Okay."

Pop got in his truck and drove away.

The next day I went to see Pop at his mother's house. When I got there, we went outside to talk.

Pop said, "Why is your mother afraid of me?"

"Pop, you know the answer to that question."

"I don't know why she is afraid of me. I haven't done anything. A lot of people, including the police are putting ideas in her head. Do you think I am guilty?"

"Pop, I wasn't here when it happened, and all I know is what I have heard."

"What have you heard?"

"It looks like you are guilty."

"Never mind what you have heard for now. Do you think I had anything to do with your grandparents' deaths?"

"No."

"You have to convince your mother. I asked her to come home, and she refused. You know how people talk, and most of the time, they don't have a clue about the truth. Why would I kill your grandparents? I know who started this gossip. It was probably Allison and her dumb husband. He is the one that sent my daughter to get you and call the police on me."

"Pop, you can't just show up any time you want. They have a restraining order against you. If you come there again, I am sure you will be arrested."

"You know, it is a damn shame a man can't see his own family. Do you think you could convince your mom to come over to see me?"

"No, Pop. There is no way Mom is coming over here."

"Okay. I want you to write a letter for me. You write better than I do. Make sure you give it to her. Talk to her and tell her she doesn't have anything to fear from me."

"Okay, Pop. I will."

I knew there was no chance in hell Mom would come see him or move back in with him.

When I got home, I gave Mom the letter. She read it and threw it in the trashcan.

"Are you going to go see him?" I asked.

"The next time I see him, it will be with my attorney. He sold our property without me signing anything. I don't know much about the law, but I am sure he can't do that. Would you watch the kids tomorrow? Allison and I are going to see if we can find someone to take my case. I am sorry that you have to be caught up in this mess."

"It's all right, Mom. It's not your fault. Only one person caused this. I said I am glad you are going with Allison. I don't think you should go alone.

"Don't worry."

The last couple of days had been very difficult. I thought the worst was behind us, but it looked like we were in for a rough road. I hated lying to Pop, but I couldn't see any other choice. I thought I had made the right one. I had never seen Pop so undecided. He looked like he didn't know what to do. He was always so sure of himself. I wished I could help him, but I couldn't. I felt the walls closing in on me again. I needed time to regroup. Maybe I would go to the Flamingo Club tonight. When Mom got home later that day, she seemed happier. Having someone looking out for her interests made her feel a lot better.

That night, I went to the Flamingo Club and had a nice time. I was in worse shape than I thought. I didn't usually drink, so after two drinks, I began to get a buzz. I decided to go home and sleep it off. As I was leaving, I saw two old friends. One said, "I would have never expected you boys to turn out like this." I was so embarrassed. I wanted to say I wasn't normally like this, but it was too late. This was the image he would have of me for the rest of his life. How could I have been so stupid? I would have to find him and explain if I could. It was an eye-opener for me. Never again would I allow myself to get that drunk. Last year hadn't been a very good year for me, and it looked like this one wouldn't be any better.

The next day, Mom and Allison found a lawyer. It looked like we would have someone to defend us. I felt a lot better, and I was sure Mom did, too. She was spending a lot of time with our relatives. At least she had someone to talk to. She had been acting more herself the last day or two. She seemed to know what she needed to do.

Early that morning, there was a fire about two blocks away. Our landlady came over and said, "I am sorry."

I didn't understand. I told her we were okay, but I was a little confused as to why she was sorry. She said, "I know you and your family have a hard time seeing homes burning down."

That evening, I was supposed to take my girlfriend to a basketball game at the school. She couldn't make it, so I went by myself. On my way home there were about ten people walking behind me, talking very loud. It sounded like an argument. One of the girls said, "Forget it, you creep. I am going to walk with Bryant." She ran to catch up with me and introduce herself.

She said, "My name is Mary."

When we got near my street, I told her that I would be turning off at the next street.

She said, "Aren't you going to walk me home?"

Being a gentleman, I walked her home.

A couple of days later, I went out looking for a job. On my way home, Pop pulled up beside me in his truck and told me to get in. He was still upset about being told he couldn't visit us unless he had permission from Mom. "I want you to write another letter for me," he said.

I wrote the letter for him then he asked me to read it back to him. I guess he wanted to be sure what I had written. When I got home, I gave it to Mom. She balled it up and put in the trash without even reading it.

"Mom, aren't you going to read it?"

"No, I am not interested in anything he has to say. Did you write it for him?"

"Yes. He is saying the same thing—that he is innocent. What did your attorney say? Does she think we have a case?"

"She seems to think so, but she wanted to do a little research before we decide what to do."

After living in Tallulah for a month or so, I got so homesick that I needed to go back to Henderson.

"You are not going to stay all night there, are you?" asked Mom when I told her.

"No, I just want to check on the house."

"Okay, but do not stay too long."

It was just an excuse to go see Laverne. I think Mom knew my motive because she smiled as I walked out the door. It was good to see home again. Before I got to Laverne's house, I met up with a couple of the guys.

Charles said, "If you came to see Laverne, it is too late. She left for Los Angeles a couple days ago."

"I didn't come to Henderson for that," I lied. I felt stupid that I hadn't let her know where I was. I talked to the guys for a while then I left to go see the house. I went next door to see Wilbur first; to my disappointment, he wasn't home. Pop's truck was parked out front. If I went in, I knew I would have to answer a lot of questions, but I had to go by if I wanted to see Bull Face. As I walked up the driveway, he started barking then ran and jumped on me. He ran around the house, and I played with him for a long time before I went inside. He was as happy to see me, as I was to see him, but I knew this might be the last time I would see my dog.

When I got inside, Pop was surprised to see me. He asked me to come in and stay for a while. We made a lot of small talk, but we didn't have the kind of conversation a father and son should have. It was almost as if we had to censor what we said to one another. It was getting late, and I had to go. He wanted me to stay, have dinner with him, and spend the night, but that was impossible. I told him I had to get back to Tallulah.

"What's wrong with *you?*" Pop asked. "Are *you* afraid of me or something?"

"No, but Mom will be worried if I don't come home."

"What is she worried about? No one is trying to harm her. Okay, *you* can go, but I want *you* to write another letter for me first."

I hated writing the letter because I knew Mom would just throw it away. I wanted to tell him writing letters wasn't helping, but I didn't say anything. I told him I would give Mom the letter as soon as I got home. It was hard seeing Pop so sad, but what could I do? I had pledged my allegiance to Mom. I told him I would see him later and left. I knew he was angry with me again.

When I got outside, Bull Face was waiting, wagging his tail in excitement. I sat down with him because I knew it might be the last time. I told him I couldn't take him with me because he was a country dog and used to roaming for miles every day. If he went to the city, he would be restricted to an area about fifty feet square. Sooner or later, he would venture into the street and probably be hit by a car. I told him he was better off in the country and that Wilbur would take care of him. I hugged him and said goodbye. He tried to follow me, whimpering as if he knew I was saying goodbye. I told him go back and started running. When I looked back, he was standing in the road. He started barking, and I put my hands over my ears and ran as hard and fast as I could. I had no idea how hard it was to say goodbye to a pet. Tears ran down my face. I was leaving him, but it was for the best thing. Even if I took him to Tallulah, we would only be there until the trial was over. I knew he didn't understand, but it was best for him. I felt as though I had deserted him. What the hell was wrong with me? I couldn't get anything right. I had to get over this feeling before I got to Tallulah because Mom needed me to be strong. I couldn't let her see me like this.

I decided not to go back to Henderson anymore. It had a bad effect on me. I thought I could find refuge; instead, it was stressful, and the memories were exhausting. I had to find a way to get Henderson out of my mind, or I wouldn't be any good to anyone. Everywhere I went was more pain and sorrow. What the hell had I done to deserve this? I had to find another way to relax.

When I got home, Mom asked if I had seen Pop while I was there.

"He asked me to stay the night, but I told him I couldn't. He wasn't too happy with the idea, but there wasn't anything he could do."

"Did you see Laverne?"

"No, she had left for California."

The next day, our attorney told Mom she would contact Pop concerning her portion of the money from the sale of our property. Pop's lawyer had been stalling with excuse after excuse. Now that we had a lawyer, maybe Pop's lawyer would stop stalling. Pop's lawyer sent word that he would be willing to give her some of the money if she would meet with him. Mom said there was no way she was going to do that. She contacted her lawyer, who said, "Don't worry. He has to give you your portion of the money. It is the law." Weeks passed and nothing happened.

Finally, we decided to see him, with the condition that I would be with her. I don't think Pop knew that until he saw me.

"Why did you bring Bryant?" Pop asked. "I thought we were going to go off together and discuss our problems."

"I just came to get my money and nothing else," said Mom.

He gave her some, but not all that he owed her. Mom was a little upset, but at least she knew now that it was just a ploy to see her. For a while, it looked like things were about to escalate out of control. They were arguing, and it didn't sound good. Finally, he gave her an envelope, and Mom walked away. It wasn't a total loss, as she had some money at last, but it was obvious that they would never be able to settle this on their own. Mom's lawyer wasn't doing a very good job. On our way home, I could tell that Mom was a little shook up.

She said, "That was a mistake. I won't meet with him again without my attorney."

Mom was still upset when we got home, so I stayed around the house for the next week or so. After a while, she began to calm down, although sometimes I heard her crying at night. I knew how she felt. I had done more crying in the last three months than I had in the first eighteen years of my life.

One day, Mom said, "Bryant, why don't you go out and have a little fun? I am okay, and I am not going anywhere. Go on out and have some fun with your friends. Don't worry about me. I will be all right."

"Are you sure?"

"Yes, now get out of here."

I called my new girlfriend and asked if she wanted to go the movies. She said yes, but that she had some homework to do, and would meet me at the school. I waited and waited. Finally, the usher said, "Ten minutes before the start of the movie."

Mary walked up and said, "Waiting for someone?"

"Yes."

She decided to keep me company until my girlfriend got to the school. After a while, I realize she wasn't coming. I started walking toward the auditorium where the movie was showing.

"Are you going to walk away from me like that?" asked Mary.

I had forgotten she was waiting with me. I guess I was so upset that I wasn't thinking. "I'm sorry. I wasn't thinking. Would you like to be my guest?"

"Yes, I would like that."

We went inside a little early so we could get good seats. For some reason, people started throwing things in the auditorium. It got so bad that we had to crawl on the floor to keep from being hit. I was so pissed off I just wanted to hit somebody. After we got outside, I met up with one of my friends. We wanted to go back inside and knock some heads together, but we changed our minds because we had girls with us. My first night out in a long time, and this happened! We decided to go to the sandwich shop. Later that evening, I was walking Mary home when a familiar truck passed. It was Pop's truck, and he was headed towards our house.

I guess my expression changed, because Mary said, "Is everything okay?"

"Yes," I answered.

Inside, my heart was beating like mad. I started walking a little faster. Mary had trouble keeping up with me.

"Is something wrong?"

I lied and said, "I forgot that my aunt was coming over tonight. She wanted to talk to me."

"Okay, I know that that isn't true, but you can tell me later."

"Thank you. I will talk to you later."

After she got inside her house, I ran as fast as I could. By the time I got home, I was soaked and exhausted, but everything was okay. The next day, Mom and the kids went to Aunt Allison's house for a visit. I decided to go downtown, look around, and try to meet some girls. I saw some old classmates that I hadn't seen for a long time. On my way home, Pop pulled up beside me and asked me to get in the truck.

Pop said, "Has your Momma thought about what I said in the letter?"

"She hasn't said anything to me."

"Did you ask her?"

"No."

"Then how do you know?"

"She would have said something if she had a message for you."

"I want you to write another letter."

After I finished writing the letter for him, we talked for a while, and then I got out of the truck and left. I wasn't sure I should give the letter to Mom. She never read them anyway. When Mom got home, I gave it to her, and as usual, she threw it away without reading it.

"From now on," Mom said, "any time he sends a letter, just throw it away. I am not interested in anything he has to say."

The next day, Mary and I were taking a stroll when Pop pulled up beside me again, wanting to talk. I told Mary who he was and asked her to wait for me until I wrote another letter for him. I wrote as fast as I could, and when I finished, I read it back to him. That wasn't enough. He wanted to talk, too. He leaned out of the truck and told Mary she could go. I was mad. Instead of talking to my girl, I had to listen to him talk about the same old damn thing again. After about an hour, he finally had said everything on his mind. When I got home, I threw the letter in the trash. I knew Mom didn't want to read it. I went to the phone booth, as we did not have a phone in our new house yet, called Mary, and apologized for having to leave her like that.

She said, "It was okay, but your father sounds mean."

"He can be sometimes."

"I hope this doesn't happen all the time."

"No, and that is the last time that will ever happen."

I went home and told Mom about the letter.

Mom said, "Did you throw it away?"

"Yes, just as soon as I got home."

The next day, Mom said, "I have some papers for you to sign."

"What kind of papers?" I asked.

"It's a signature card, just in case you need to get money out of the bank."

"You don't need to do that."

"Yes, I do, in case you need some money for one reason or another. The bank manager said it would be wise to have two people on the account, in case of an emergency."

"Okay."

I knew it was more than just that. I signed the paper to make her feel more comfortable. The following day, I took the signed paper back to the bank. I had to sign another paper to confirm the signature. Just my luck, on my way home, Pop caught me again.

"What did your Momma say?" he asked.

"About what?"

"What do you think?"

I was tired of lying to him, so I told him the truth about the letters. He got so angry that even I was scared.

"You mean to tell me that all those letters I had you writing she didn't even bother to read?"

"Yes," I answered.

"Why haven't told me this before?"

"I was hoping you would stop sending her letters. That way, no one would get hurt."

"What is wrong with her? She acts like she is afraid of me."

"She is."

"What have I ever done to her?"

"Nothing, Pop."

"When you were living at home, did you ever see me hit her or anything?"

"No, Pop."

"Of course you haven't. In all the years we were together I never hit her, not even once."

"I know, Pop."

"Who is putting these ideas in her head? Does it make sense for her to be afraid of me?"

"Pop, if *you* think *you* will get back together with Mom, I should tell *you*—it will never happen."

"Why not?"

"She thinks *you* killed her parents."

"That is a lie! I didn't do anything to her parents."

"It doesn't matter what I think or what *you* think. The only thing that matters is what Mom thinks, and she thinks *you* are guilty, and she is afraid of *you*. She thinks *you* might try to harm her."

"If I wanted to do something to her, I could. I could walk up to that house and kill her, and no one would know who did it."

I paused before I spoke. I knew what I wanted to say, but it didn't come out the way I intended. "If *you* did that, *you* better make sure *you* get me, too, because I would find *you* and do the same to *you*."

He just looked at me for about ten seconds. "You said enough! Get *your* ass out of my truck."

I couldn't believe what I had just said. I wanted to take the words back as soon as I said them, but it was too late. For the first time, Pop didn't look at me as if I was his son or even a family member. He looked at me as if he didn't know me. It was frightening. He had the coldest eyes I had ever seen. I didn't say anything else; I just got out of the truck. He took one last look at me and drove away.

Chapter 10

What Had I Done?

When I got home, I went to my bedroom and sat down, regretting what I had just said to Pop. Mom knew something was wrong and came to my room.

"What is wrong?" she asked.

"Nothing."

"Come on, Bryant. I know when something is wrong with my children."

I told her what had happened, and she said, "I am sorry you got caught in the middle of your parents' problems, but it is done now. Just forget about it. Worrying will do you no good. Thank you for standing up for me."

"I didn't have a choice. It happened before I knew it. When I realized what I said, it was too late."

"Don't worry. He won't hold it against you."

"I am not so sure of that. I hope we don't see any strange men coming up our walkway. They might get their halos shot off."

We laughed and tried to joke about it. I guess that was our way of relieving the stress that had been building up for weeks. I didn't sleep much that night. It had gotten to the point I didn't recognize myself anymore. I had just threatened the man I respected and loved most on this planet. Was he my father or the enemy?

I decided for the next couple of days to take a different route home to avoid running into Pop. It was all I could think of to avoid a confrontation. It wouldn't take much to start an all-out war. If it came to that, none of us would survive. No matter how it ended, all of us would lose. It was better to keep the uneasy truce in place. I had hoped Mom's attorney would create a calm atmosphere, but she was only making things worse in some ways. Mom went to meet her attorney to discuss strategy, but the attorney had invited opposing council and my father. Any confidence we had flew out the door. You shouldn't invite opposing council to a strategy meeting. I didn't know if she was incompetent or just evil. Either way, we needed another attorney.

The following days were spent looking for another attorney. Aunt Allison recommended someone in the banking profession. When Mom told him what happened, he asked who our attorney was. After Mom told him, he put his hands to his face and shook his head. That told Mom all she needed to know. Mom fired her attorney the next day and hired one recommended by her advisor. I wasn't sure this one would be any better, but he couldn't be worse. Mom had chosen the female attorney, thinking she would be more sensitive to her problems. One of the first things the new attorney said was that she wasn't to meet with her husband or his attorney under any condition. If there were to be a meeting, he would inform her ahead of time. Even then, it was possible she wouldn't have to be there. Finally, we had an attorney who seemed to know what he was doing. That afternoon, I decided to go see Mary.

"Is everything okay?" she asked when she saw me.

"Yes, it is much better than before."

"Can you tell me what was wrong?"

"Did you hear about the murder of two people in East Carroll Parish?"

"Yes, but I didn't think much about it."

"The two people that were murdered were my grandparents, and my father is the prime suspect."

"Is that why he is always trying to get you to write letters for him?"

"Yes. He hopes to get my Mom back, but that is never going to happen."

"No wonder you are always so sad."

"I am not sad all that much."

"Yes, you are; maybe more than you think. I knew something was wrong because you are always looking behind you as if you are looking for someone. Do you think he is guilty?"

"Yes, he is guilty, just as sure as the sun rises in the east and sets in the west. If not, he is the product of the greatest conspiracy since the death of John F Kennedy."

"I am so sorry for you," said Mary.

"Don't be. We will get through this as we have everything else. The worst thing is to wake up one day and realize that the man you have lived with all your life is someone you don't really know."

The following day, I decided to go see David at my grandmother's house. I told him Mom had a new attorney.

"Why does she need an attorney?"

"Pop wouldn't give Mom any of the money he got from the sale of the property. He gave her some the other day, but not all that is due her. Has Pop asked you a lot of questions?"

"No, not too many."

"Can you keep our conversation confidential?"

"No problem," said David.

Grandmother came into the living room. "Your mother should give Edwin another chance," she said. "He is innocent."

I remembered a time when she thought he was guilty, but it was her son, and she was going to defend him whether he was guilty or not. She tried desperately to convince me of his innocence. Maybe she was trying to convince herself. I understood exactly how she felt, as just a few weeks ago I felt the same way. But sooner or later, you have to accept things the way they are.

I said goodbye to everyone and went home to see if everything was still all right.

The next day, it happened. I saw Pop! He pulled up beside me and asked me to get in. I got in the truck, not knowing what would happen next.

"Why don't we just forget about what happen the other day?" he said.

"That's all right with me."

He was as depressed as I was. He sounded desperate. We discussed what had happened between him, Mom, and their lawyers. He said they had wanted to solve the problem before it got out of hand. Sometimes I looked at him and wanted to say, "Pop, it is going to be okay." Although I knew that wasn't the truth, I felt sorry for him. I couldn't imagine the pain he must have been going through. Sometimes he acted as if he wanted to say something to me but didn't know how. I was afraid of what he wanted to say. If he just came out and said, "I did it," I didn't know if my heart could handle it. I loved my parents and having to decide between the two was almost unbearable. I wanted to know the truth, and I didn't want to know. Either way, it wasn't going to turn out good for me. What if he said, "Son, I did it, and I need your help to stay out of jail and won't bother your mother, so it comes down to me or your grandparents. Who do you care for most?" I hoped I would never be in that position. Even through I knew he was guilty, sometimes I wanted to defend him because he was my pop, but I couldn't. After I wrote the letter for him, we talked briefly, and then I left. He seemed so sincere defending himself that I wondered if we all were wrong.

When I got home, I told Mom I had talked with Pop.

"Is he still angry with you?" she asked.

"I don't think so. He still claims he is innocent."

"Do you believe him?"

"I wish he was innocent, but I know different. I would kill for it to be anyone but him."

"I know, son, but he put us in this situation."

Several days later, I was talking to Mary. "Are you sure he is guilty?" she asked.

"I hate to say it, but yes, I think he is guilty."

"Has he done anything bad before?"

"No," I said, but that was a lie.

For the first time, I started thinking about the past. He had a pattern of being lawless. I remember Pop running into the house and telling Mom that the tractor was on fire. A few days later, the insurance agent came out and looked at it. According to Pop, the insurance agent was upset because he thought Pop could have put the fire out. Pop said, "I told him I was afraid the gas tank would explode." The insurance agent had to pay him for the tractor. Pop was happy to get that check.

When we purchased our property, it had a house on it. Several years later, Pop came home and told us the house on the property had burned down. Once again, Pop got an insurance check. If I had noticed the pattern, I was sure the police would also. Maybe all these accidents were just coincidental. Whom was I kidding? I didn't believe that, and I didn't think anyone else would, either. You tried it one time too many, Pop.

I started changing my route from home to avoid seeing Pop. I hated myself for doing it, but I didn't want to lie to him anymore. With my limited options, I decided to hide instead. I wished I could go somewhere to relax for a while. I couldn't even walk down the street without being harassed. After living in Tallulah for about two and a half months, David was tired of the whole mess, so he went to Milwaukee. I envied him. I wished I had somewhere to go for peace and quiet.

Mom started going to her cousin's house for a little down time. One evening in March, she made arrangements to go to their house, but she changed her mind. The next day, Mom's cousin came by and said she had seen Mr. Smith riding up and down the street most of the night.

"Are you sure it was him?" asked Mom.

"Yes, I am sure it was him," answered her cousin.

"It is a good thing I didn't come over last night," said Mom.

"God must be on your side. Can you imagine what could have happened had he caught you out on the street alone?"

After our cousin left, Mom said, "It almost seems as if he was expecting to see me."

We began to wonder if someone was telling him about Mom's plans. But who? "Did you tell anyone else you were going over to our cousin's house?" I asked Mom.

Mom couldn't remember. Either way, she would have to be careful from now on. Somehow, it didn't seem like things were getting any better.

That weekend, my cousin Watson came home from college. We went out and had a good time together. We avoided discussing the problems in our family. I guess we were both afraid of offending one another. His father and mine were eternal enemies. After a good night out on the town, we went to the outskirts of town and had a long talk.

"Why did you want to go out and party with me?" I asked him.

"You are my cousin and one my best friends."

"Maybe. But my father was the one responsible for all the trouble."

"We will let our parents solve their problems, and that won't affect us."

After we talked that night, we never brought it up again. For the next two months, we painted the town red every chance we got.

My girlfriend was a little upset that Watson and I were having a good time together. I was spending a lot of time with him, and she didn't like it at all.

"We have been so depressed these last four months," I said. "We had to blow off some steam."

"I don't mind," she said. "That I just want to be included."

The next week, she came over and took my sisters to the movies. From that day on, my sisters were always talking about what a good girl she was. I agreed that she was a great girlfriend.

Chapter 11

The Trial Begins

We were told the trial would be in April. I was glad we were finally getting to the end of this nightmare.

The next time I saw Pop, he asked me about my girlfriend. "What are you doing with that white man's daughter?"

"Her father is Mexican. He is not white."

"Well she looks white to me."

I didn't want to get into a fight with him about something so stupid so I ignored him.

"Has your mother changed her mind?" he asked me.

"No, Pop. I don't think she will ever change her mind."

"You know she is going to put me in jail."

"Pop, if you are innocent, you won't go to jail."

"Are you kidding? What are people going to think when they learn my wife is testifying against me?"

"I am sorry, Pop, but there is nothing I can do."

"Will you try to talk some sense into your mom?"

"Yes, Pop. I will do my best, but don't expect too much. She has made her mind up."

That weekend, Watson and I were supposed to go out and have some fun, but he was having finals at college, so he couldn't make it. I decided to go out anyway. When I got to the club, one of my old friends was there, and we had a stupendous time. Maybe too good of a time. My friend got so drunk he went into the ladies' bathroom by mistake. Before we realized what had happened, the police were coming through the door. Someone had called the cops. He asked my friend to go outside, and I went with him because I knew he couldn't explain. He was too drunk.

The police officer asked, "Which of you idiots went into the ladies' bathroom?"

I paused before I answered, as I didn't want to tell on my friend. Before I could think of what to say, Elgin said, "Me."

"Are you crazy or something?" asked the officer. "Didn't you know that going into the ladies' is against the law?"

"Sorry, Officer, he made a mistake," I said. "The bathrooms are side by side, and he is a little drunk. He didn't go in the girl's bathroom on purpose; it was a mistake."

The officer said, "How would you feel if someone walked in on your sister or girlfriend?"

"I wouldn't like it."

"Of course you wouldn't like it."

"Officer," I said, "it will not happen again. We are leaving as soon as we finish here."

"It is too late for that."

"I am classified 1A, and so is my friend. We will probably be in Vietnam in a couple of months. As a matter of fact, he has orders to report for his physical in three weeks. We were just having a little fun before we were drafted. This was our way of saying goodbye. We would like to think we will live through it, but it is possible that one or both of us won't be coming back."

The officer was beginning to feel sorry for us. He looked at his partner. "Okay, I will overlook it this time. I will give you a warning this time, but if I have to come out here again, somebody is going to jail!"

"Don't worry," I said. "We are going home."

"Okay, I will let you go this time, but you should be ashamed of yourselves. Drunk in public. Try to conduct yourselves like men."

"Thank you, Officer."

The cops got in their squad car and left.

Elgin said, "What the hell were you talking about? I am not classified 1A; I am classified 1F."

"Stupid. I had to tell the man something."

We went home. That was enough for one night. I helped my friend home and then headed home myself.

On my way home, I passed the club and saw several of my buddies leaving. We laughed about what had happened earlier. We were a little intoxicated and loud. When we got close to my house, wouldn't you know it, my landlady turned on her porch light and started yelling at us to be quiet. One of my buddies said, "That old lady is crazy. Let's teach her a lesson." We picked up some rocks and bottles and threw them at her house. I didn't realize it would make so much noise. It scared the hell out of her. She closed the door and turned off all the lights. We started running because we knew she would be calling the police. I ran about five blocks past my home to my friend's house. I didn't want her to know I had anything to do with throwing the rocks and bottles. About twenty minutes later, I quietly returned home.

The next morning, I told Mom what we had done. Mom said, "Bryant, you should be ashamed of yourself."

"I was sick of that woman complaining about everything, so we taught her a lesson."

Mom turned around and walked away, doing her best not to laugh. Later that morning, our landlady came over and told us about the boys that threw rocks at her house. She asked if I had seen anyone walking down the street last night. I told her I had come home early. I sat and listened to her lie about what happened. According to her, there were about ten boys running down the street throwing glass at all the houses. She told them to be quiet, and they ran off when they saw her porch light come on. I wanted to complain that that wasn't how it happened, but it would have only made things worse for Mom. I hoped she got some satisfaction out of lying!

Later that week, the police came by our house early in the morning. One officer said, "We came by to let you know that your husband's bail has been revoked. The trial is in a couple of weeks, and the district attorney didn't want him to skip bail. It is standard procedure. This is only to insure that he is here for the trial. Some people have been known to run when they don't think they will win their case. This is not to say he is innocent or guilty; it's just a precaution."

We thanked him for letting us know. We were fast approaching the end of this nightmare. It was hard to tell if Mom was happy or sad. I, for one, was happy we were almost at the end.

After the police left, Mom said, "I want you to promise that no matter what happens you won't split the children up. If something happens, I want you to be their guardian. You are almost nineteen years old now, and you could take care of them if something happened to me."

"Mom, don't talk like that. Nothing is going to happen to you."

"People are capable of doing terrible things when their backs are against the wall."

I didn't know what to say. She had caught me off guard.

"You promise to keep the children together?" she asked.

"Sure, Mom. I will make sure the children grow up in the same house."

You would think hearing that Pop had been put back in jail would have made her feel better. It seemed to have had the opposite affect.

The next day, I went to tell Grandmother that Pop had been arrested again. She wasn't happy. She didn't understand why they put him in jail again. I wanted to explain, but I knew it wouldn't make any difference. The only thing on her mind was that her son had been arrested. I guess if it were my son, I would feel the same way. I felt sorry for Grandmother because I knew there was no way Pop would be found innocent. She was in for a rough road. I almost hated to see her reaction when he was put in jail for years. I knew it would break her heart, but there was nothing I could do. I was largely responsible for his being arrested. She would hate my guts if she knew. I tried to console her, but crying was the order for this day. I hoped I would not have to testify at the trial. It would be a dagger in Grandmother's heart if I testified against Pop. She asked if I was going to go see him and told me to tell him she would do all she could to help him. When I got home, Mom asked me how Momma Givens had taken the news.

I said, "About as well as can be expected."

The next day, I went to see Pop. I wasn't sure why I was going to see him or what I was going to say. What if he asked if I were going to testify against him? I hoped I wouldn't have to. It would be hard as hell to get up in court and point the finger at my own dad. Mom would have to testify, though. I was nervous when I got to the court-house, but visiting hours were over.

One of the officers said, "You can go around to the outside to talk to him. If you call him from the grounds outside, he might hear you."

I went outside and called Pop, and just as the officer said, he answered. He talked about the upcoming trial and said again that he was innocent. While we were talking, I heard someone call my name. I recognized the voice. It was one of my classmates, Ronald Jenkins.

Roland said, "Are you going back to Los Angeles?"

"Yes," I said. "I will be going back right after the trial."

Roland said he had been born in Los Angeles, but he had lived most of his life in Louisiana.

I guess Pop got a little upset with me talking to Ronald. "Did you come here to talk to me or him?" he asked.

I put an end to Ronald's conversation as soon as possible.

"I have something I want you to do for me," said Pop. "A friend of mine will be coming by the house to borrow some tools." I was to go with his friend and let him have the tools, but only the ones Pop told me to let him have. He was not to get anything else.

"When is your friend coming by?" I asked.

"Probably in about a week."

"I will take care of it."

"Is your mom is still listening to all the gossip?"

"What gossip are you talking about, Pop?"

"You know damn well what gossip I am talking about, boy."

I had pissed him off. I would have to choose my words more carefully. The last thing I wanted to do was get him even more upset. "You know what Mom thinks."

Pop's reply was, as usual, that everybody was against him. He had forgotten that he put us in this position. I didn't know what else to say so I said goodbye and left it at that.

When I returned home, I told Grandmother I had gone to see Pop and he was all right. I suppose it gave her some comfort, but I am sure she knew there was no hope for Pop. Secretly, I hoped there was a way for Pop to get out of this mess and still make everyone happy. However, looking at the facts, there was no chance of that happening. I told Mom about my conversation with Pop and Grandmother. We sat for hours discussing what to do next. We really wanted to resolve the conflict, but it was out of our hands.

The next day, when we all had calmed down, we tried to look at the facts rationally. When we went to court, we had to be sure we were giving facts, not our personal opinions. We went over it repeatedly, and it always came out the same way. Pop was the only one that could have committed the murders. I hated that all the facts led to Pop. I guess I was waiting for some ninth-hour solution like always happened on *Perry Mason*. Unfortunately, this was not a television show, and not all the characters got to go home afterwards.

I thought we had done a very good job of putting the facts together. There was one thing we still didn't allow ourselves to think about. What if he were found innocent? That would really mess things up. I knew Mom wouldn't go back to him, but she couldn't just leave the state with his children. He would fight her tooth and nail for the kids. If that happened, what in the name of God would I do? Would I stay with her or go back to Los Angeles? There was no future in being a small farmer and I couldn't just get back on the bus and go back to Los Angeles. I had two options, and I didn't like either one of them. What if I went back to Los Angeles and something happened? Could I live with myself? What had seemed so simple a few hours ago didn't seem so simple anymore. Maybe I was just making myself crazy. I had to stop looking for problems.

Just when I thought I had all the facts, Mom completely destroyed it in a matter of seconds. During one of her conversations with Pop, he said, "You think you have all the answers, don't you? You are Miss Goody Two Shoes, and you couldn't do anything wrong if your life counted on it. Well, the world isn't like that. A lot of people do whatever they have to in order to get what they want. When we get to court, you are going to find out there is a lot more to this than meets the eye. There is a lot going on you don't know about. When it comes out what really happened a lot of people are going to be surprised. I want to see the expression on your face." I was almost afraid to ask Mom about some of these other things, but I had to.

"That is what has been bothering me, too," Mom said. "Maybe he is not in this by himself."

"Mom, I know Pop. There is no way he would put himself in a predicament like this, where someone else would know what he did. He is too private. Conspiracy is not his cup of tea. If he is involved, you can be sure he acted alone. Who on Henderson would get involved with something like that, anyway? Good Christian people live on Henderson."

"How do you know they are from Henderson?"

"Because those are the people he knows the best, and I know the people on Henderson."

"Are you sure?"

"Of course I am sure; we have wonderful people on Henderson."

Mom moved forward, put her arms around my neck, and whispered in my ear to keep anyone else from hearing what she had to say. "The last time I talked to Betty, she told me she got a letter from some of our Christian friends here on Henderson, and if we gave them two thousand dollars, they would see to it that Edwin disappeared."

"What do you mean 'disappear'?"

Mom just looked at me.

"Do you know who they are?" I asked.

"Yes." Then she told me who "they" were.

I couldn't believe what I was hearing. My legs felt weak so I sat on the edge of the sofa. "Mom, are they going to give them the money?"

"No, they want two thousand dollars up front before they do the job. Betty was afraid they might take the money and not keep their promise. It might be a scam. Plus, we paid a lot of money for the funeral, the trip home, and the holidays, and money is in short supply now."

"I am sorry. I didn't know."

"I know, but you had to be told. I wanted to tell you earlier, but I was waiting for the right time."

It was almost unbelievable that we had hit men and murderers on Henderson. You really don't know people; you just think you do. With this new information, a lot of things made sense. This was why Mom had been so worried. If someone had offered to kill Pop for a price, would someone have offered to kill Mom for a price? Somehow, I didn't feel so safe anymore. Maybe that was why Mom made me promise to keep the kids together if something happened to her. Although we were at the end, it could be very bloody. I don't think the kids had much to worry about, but I was not sure about Mom. What if he decided she had to disappear?

In a couple of days, Pop's friend came by to pick up the tools and equipment. Of all the nights to come, he had to come when I had company. He even brought another guy with him. I told Mary I had to do something for Pop and would be back in an hour or so. I told Mom I was going to Henderson to get the tools for Pop's friend. She said okay, but I could see the concern in her face.

When we got to Henderson, I told the two men to stay outside and I would be right back. I went into the house and got the keys to the tool shed. Then I opened the shed and gave him the tools. He started to pick up some of the other tools, and I told him he could only take the tools Pop told me to give to him. He tried to tell me the tools were part of the equipment, but I knew better. I had been using them for years. He laughed and said, "I wanted to see what I could get away with."

We put the equipment and tools in the back of the truck and started home. Thank God Bull Face wasn't there. I didn't want to go through that again. As we left, I took a last look at our home. I really loved that house. On our way back to Tallulah, a chill came over me. If they wanted to do something to Mom, tonight would be the perfect time. Maybe this was part of the plan. Get me out of the house so Mom would be by herself.

I had fallen for the oldest trick in the world. Divide and conquer. How could I have been so gullible? My brain seemed to have gone into overdrive. If they tried something tonight, what could I do? I was sitting between two men, not a good position to be in. I needed to come up with a plan that might work if I had to defend myself. I pulled out my keys as if I wanted to use the fingernail clippers. I decided I'd rake one's face with my keys, elbow the other in the throat, and push him out the door. That would give me enough time get out of the truck, make my escape, call Mom, and tell her to get out of the house. If they decided to act, it would probably happen between Sondheimer and Tallabena. There weren't many people that lived along this stretch of highway. It was mostly abandoned homes and woods. As we approach the area, I expected them to make their move, so I prepared myself mentally. We passed that stretch of highway without anything happening.

When we reached the outskirts of Tallulah, I knew I had let my imagination run away with me. I felt like an ass thinking Mr. James Kelly would be part of a conspiracy to hurt Mom. I had known this man most of my life. What the hell was I thinking? Although we had been talking all the way home, I couldn't remember a word he had said. I was too busy thinking of ways to hurt him.

Mr. Kelly asked, "Do you know where your girlfriend is?"

"Yes, I do," I said.

"I bet she is out with some other guy."

"No chance of that."

"Are you sure? She could have been with anyone while you were gone."

"I know exactly where she is."

"Where?"

"She is at my house."

"How do you know?"

"Because she was at my house when you came by."

"You left that pretty little girl to come with us?"

"Pop told me to give you the equipment and tools he had promised to let you use."

"Thank you, but I wouldn't have left that pretty little girl to go with a couple of hard legs."

We all got a big laugh out of that. I felt a little better, but I wouldn't be completely comfortable until I got home. When we pulled up in front of our house, I could see the kids through the window playing inside. Only then did I feel relieved. I had almost given myself a heart attack worrying about what had happened while I was gone.

Chapter 12

The Day of Truth

It was finally the day of truth, only a matter of hours before we started to unravel what had happened four months ago. I had been waiting for this day a very long time. Surprisingly, I was more nervous today than I had been in an eternity. Only three of us were going to the trial—Mom, Diana, and me.

When we walked into the courthouse, all eyes were on us. I didn't like being in the spotlight. We sat down somewhere near the center of the courtroom. Before we could get comfortable, one of the police officers came over and asked if we were the Smith family.

Mom said, "Yes, we are."

"There are seats reserved for you at the front of the court room. I will take you to them."

I had hoped we could melt into the crowd, but that wasn't going to happen now. We were front and center, so the whole world could see us. After we were seated, only then did I notice that a trial had started already. I wasn't sure if it was ours or someone else's.

I listened to the person testifying to see if it had anything to do with our trial. One of the witnesses mentioned he had seen two or three "niggers" talking or doing something. A hush fell over the courtroom. I couldn't believe he had used that word in the courtroom. Every face in the courtroom—eighty percent of which were black—looked angry.

"Mom, did you hear that idiot?"

"Don't worry about that. We have more important things to think about."

He looked familiar. I thought I had seen him before. He might have been the brother of a man Pop used to work for. While I tried to remember who he was, Pop walked into the courtroom with his lawyer. He wasn't wearing any restraints. He sat directly in front of us and turned to say hello. Mom was a nervous sitting so close to him.

From the time he walked in the courtroom, I couldn't remember any other testimony. All my focus was on him. After an hour or so, Pop's attorney asked for a recess, and we all got up and went outside to stretch our legs. When we get outside, I heard someone call my name. I turned around; it was one of my classmates.

"What are you doing up here?" she asked.

"I am here for a trial. I am one of the principals."

"Please tell me you didn't do anything wrong."

"Of course not. I might have to testify, though."

"I would hate to see you in trouble with the law."

"Don't worry. I am too smart for that."

We talked about the good old days in high school for a while then she said, "Would you like to see where I live?" She pointed to a house a half-mile away.

"Okay, but I can't stay long."

"That's okay."

I told Mom I was going to walk a girl home but would be back in a little while.

"The trial might start soon," Mom said.

"Mom, we just got out for recess. I don't think they will be calling us back in so soon."

"All right, but don't stay too long."

This young lady had turned her back on me when I was in high school. In her defense, she had apologized for her behavior and asked my forgiveness. We had gone full circle. Maybe we could get it right this time. I didn't know that it was love; maybe I was just glad to see someone from my class. Samantha Bishop was special to me when I was in high school. Too bad she didn't feel the same way. I can't tell you the ideas running through my head. Just before we got to her house, I heard my sister calling me.

"Mom sent me to get you. The trial is starting."

I looked at Samantha and said, "I'm sorry."

"That's okay," she said. "You can come see me when the trial is over."

I hugged her. "Goodbye."

"Come see me."

I promised Samantha I would, but that was the last time I saw her.

I hurried back to the courthouse. When I got into the courtroom, Mom gave me one of those looks. You know, the kind that says, "What are you doing? We came here for a trial, not to chase girls." I was a little ashamed and knew apologizing wouldn't do any good. Although we had been told to return to the courtroom, there was nothing happening. About five minutes later, Pop's lawyer came over and said, "Mr. Smith would like to see his children."

"What does he want?" I asked.

"Mr. Smith will explain."

I wasn't sure I should go. I looked at Mom.

"It's okay," she said. "Go see what he wants."

I was a little hesitant, but I went anyway. I hoped he wasn't going to ask us to lie for him. I wouldn't, but Diana might. She was only ten years old and could easily be told what to say. I was surprised the district attorney allowed the defense to talk to possible witnesses. It looked like I was the only one that thought this was a little strange. My sister and I were taken to a room in the back where Pop was sitting in one of the chairs.

The attorney said, "I will wait outside until you are finished. After you have talked, come and get me. I will be right down the hall."

We sat at the table and waited for Pop to say what was on his mind. Finally, he said, "If I am found guilty, I will probably get the hot seat. Nine of twelve jurors would have to find me not guilty to avoid the death penalty." He stood and walked around the room rubbing his hands together. "My attorney and I have come up with another option. If I accept a plea bargain to arson, the district attorney will probably go along with it to avoid a trial. I'm not saying I am guilty of anything, but you know what kind of luck black people have in courts. They might send me to jail just because I am black. What are your thoughts about this?"

"What does your attorney think?" I asked.

"My attorney thinks it is a good idea. I know how it looks, but I have to do what I can to avoid going to jail for the rest of my life or getting the electric chair. I didn't kill anyone, but everybody thinks I did. What kind of trial do you think I am going to have?"

"I think you should take the arson plea," I said.

"I think so also. Diana, what do you think?"

Like Diana was going to say anything different.

"If we accept the plea bargain, my attorney is sure I won't get more than nine years," Pop said.

"Yes, it is a good offer," I admitted.

"I agree. Have my attorney come back."

When the attorney re-entered the room, Pop said, "We decided to accept the plea bargain."

Mr. Howard said, "I think that is a good idea. I promise you won't have to serve more than three years."

I felt a little guilty about what I had done, but there was no other choice. My aunts and uncles on my mom's side in California would not have stood for Pop being found innocent of all charges. I did what I had to do to avoid a family blood bath. They would have killed Pop, and there was no way Pop's side of the family would have stood by and done nothing. We would have made the Hatfields and the McCoys seem tame by comparison. At least this way, we might avoid another disaster. Hopefully, this would satisfy everybody. When I got back into the courtroom, I told Mom what was going to happen.

"Are you sure the district attorney is going to go along with this?" she asked.

"We will know in a few minutes."

About five minutes later, Pop and his attorney returned to the courtroom. Pop's attorney and the district attorney had a conference with the judge, who then announced that an agreement had been reached in the case against Mr. Smith. Pop stood up and pled guilty to arson. The judge asked the district attorney if he was in agreement with the plea. The district attorney said yes. The judge looked at some papers on his desk and said, "Mr. Smith pled guilty to arson and is to receive not more than nine years and not less than three years in the state penitentiary. This court is adjourned!"

I was not sure what I was expecting. I was amazed at how many people had come to the trial. After five months, it was over. The worst part was that we didn't know any more today than we had known five months ago. We would have to ponder this for the rest of our lives. I was so disillusioned about the outcome. After all the pain and suffering, this was what we got. It was a riddle wrapped in a mystery, but the not knowing was what bothered me the most.

We got in our car and headed home. You would think we would be happy, but no one showed it. When we got home, we explained what had happened to the other kids. They seemed as puzzled as we were. The most important thing was to put this behind us and move on.

I went to my grandmother's house and told her the outcome of the case. She didn't say too much, just, "At least it is over." We had a brief conversation concerning the kids and Mom. She was trying to hold back tears. I thought it would be best if I gave her time to grieve in her own way. I hugged her and told her I was sorry.

She said, "That is okay, son; he made his bed."

Later that week, I saw Mary and told her about the trial. "You don't look too happy," she said.

I told her it had been a long and grueling ordeal and would probably take some time to get back to normal.

Mary said, "Forget about the trial and think of happier times. You could just concentrate on me. That surely will bring a smile to your face."

She was right. It did make me smile. She was full of herself today. I wasn't in the best of moods for talking, so I cut our conversation short and went back home.

On my way home, I passed an area with lots of trees. It reminded me of home, so I stopped and sat down for a while. Now that I was alone, I thought about all that had happened. There was one thing I had always refused to think about. What if I were indirectly responsible for everything?

Most people thought of my pop as heartless and cold. True, he did have a hard exterior, but he also had a soft side that very few people saw. No matter what other people thought about him, he did love his family. Maybe that was the problem. He loved us too much. He knew how much I wanted to go to college. The day before I left for California, he asked me to stay one more year and help him grow another crop. I turned him down. If I had stayed, I was sure I'd be drafted before planting season started. Instead of explaining it to him, I just said no. Mistake number one.

I really wanted to join the armed forces, but Mom was afraid I would get hurt. She had good reason to think that, as the Vietnam War was in full bloom, and there was a good chance I would have ended up there. I didn't care about that; I wanted the money. The recruiter had sent me a letter telling me I could make five hundred dollars a month in the army. That would allow me to do a lot of things. I could send money home each month and have enough left over to save for myself when I got out. I never bothered to explain any of this to my parents. I hadn't even known we were in such dire straights at the time. Mistake number two. Sure, I wanted to go to California. I wanted to see the ocean, the mountains, the beaches, and all that California had to offer before I went into the armed forces, but I didn't bother to share my ideas with Pop.

Later that day, he shocked me again.

Pop said, "When you have a son, name him after your grandparent. It is old-fashioned to give your son your name."

I said I didn't like the name Archie. Furthermore, my grandfather Archie, who we called "Daddy," had told all of us never to name a child Archie, as it was a bad luck name. There had been two sons named Archie and both died before they were adults. After I said this to Pop, he smiled. Only years later did I realize he was asking me to name a son after him. I was so focused on me I hadn't heard anything but what I wanted to hear. I knew what I wanted to do, and I wasn't going to let anything or anyone interfere with my plans.

I left God out of my plans. Mistake number three. I didn't pray about my future; I just assumed he would understand. It was too important an issue to just leave it to God. He might have wanted me to do something else, but I had my own plans, and I was going to do what I wanted. This was probably the biggest mistake of all. Don't get me wrong. I believed in God and prayed every night, but when it came to my life, I didn't need any help. I could decide what I wanted to do and go after it without anyone telling me what to do. I was smart, intelligent, arrogant, and absolutely certain I would be rich someday. At least, that is how I saw myself. My parents, grandparents, and some of my teachers had told me I was smart, so how could I have thought otherwise? Maybe that was the problem. I could hear, but I wasn't listening.

Maybe if I had taken the time to listen more clearly, I could have figured out what he was trying to say. It must have been very difficult for him to talk about emotional things. I understood that because I felt the same way. Sometimes it was hard to express how you felt about someone. It was foreign to me, and I am sure it was foreign to him. It must have ripped his guts out to even bring the topic up, but you could be sure that son number three understood exactly what he was saying. The truth of the matter is that "son number three" didn't have a clue about the more important things.

As I thought back about all the things that happened before I left, it was as plain as the nose on my face that were some difficulties in Eden, but I didn't see it. He had tried his best to make things easier for me in high school by not planting cotton. He knew how much I hated picking and chopping cotton. One Saturday evening, he came into the living room where I was and asked, "Why don't you go get your driver's license? If you had your license, you could pick up your little girlfriend and go to town."

He was trying to make life better for me, but I didn't hear him. He was thinking short term, hoping to keep me home a little longer, and I was thinking long term. A Louisiana driver's license meant nothing to me because I knew I wouldn't be in Louisiana much longer.

He told me he would send me to college next year, but I was upset because I couldn't go this year and was afraid that when next year came, he would have another excuse why I couldn't go. Maybe he was telling the truth, and he would have found a way to send me to college the following year. Maybe he was trying to bribe me to stay a little longer. Maybe it was harder on him than I thought, and just maybe he just hated seeing his sons leave.

If I were analyzing this correctly, the entire tragedy could have been avoided. If I had decided to stay home, I don't think anything would have happened. If I had told him my plans, he could have hired three people to do the work of one, but I didn't take the time to explain myself. How could I have been so blind? Everyone thought he did it out of hate for his in-laws or for money. Maybe we had misread his motive. Maybe he did it out of love for his family. Maybe he did it to send one of his sons to college. It didn't excuse what he did, and I would never forgive him, but if he did it to send me to college, didn't that make me indirectly responsible?

I spent hours thinking it through, and I wasn't happy with my conclusion. The only questions were the other things he mentioned. What did he mean when he said, "There is a lot more to this than you think"? I found it hard to believe that others were involved, but I had been wrong before about a great many things. It turned out I was not as smart as I thought. I was maybe even a little dumb. I had learned much about human nature in the last few months. It was going to be hard to trust anyone again. Now I had to live with this unsolved mystery or go crazy thinking about it, and I couldn't afford that.

When I got home, Mom was next door relaying the information to her sister. I don't think anyone was happy with the ending, but it was the only ending possible. Now we could get on with our lives.

Mom decided to move to California in the next couple of months. The kids were excited about it. I would be leaving sooner than my mother and the kids, and hopefully, I could find a job before my family got out there. I hoped it would be better in California. I knew some family members wouldn't be too happy to see us. We were the wife and children of the man that killed their parents. We very well could be leaving one hell for another.

Chapter 13

A New Beginning

On my way back to California, I had two days to prepare myself for whatever happened. Surprisingly, most of my relatives seemed glad to see me. Regardless of how things turned out in California, it couldn't be any worse than it was in my hometown. I had gotten tired of the finger pointing and whispers. At least now, we could hide in the crowds. I often wondered how they felt about us back home.

Mom and the kids arrived in California in June 1970. My older brother and I were waiting for them when they got off the bus. I was glad to see their faces. They wore the biggest smiles I had ever seen. It was great to see them so happy. It was the beginning of a new life, and hopefully, this one would be a lot better than the last one.

As the years passed, I watched the kids grow into young men and women. I felt responsible for helping them as much as I could. If one of them needed money, I felt it was my responsibility to give it to them. Sometimes, when I saw my mother going through hard times, I felt as though it were my responsibility to help. Mom and the kids had to lose their way of life because I didn't do my job thirty-five years ago, not that I did anything wrong, but a fifteen-minute conversation could have changed everything.

If there were a moral to this story, it would be, "Kids, talk to your parents and listen." You just never know when a ten or fifteen-minute conversation might save you a lifetime of regret.

As a parent, I know we keep much from our children. We want them to be happy and will do all we can to accomplish that. Whatever you do, don't leave God out of your life. Maybe, just maybe, if I had, things would have been better. Don't end up like me, thirty-five years later, wondering, "What if?"

I made my mistakes, and now I have to live with them. If you found yourself in a similar situation, what would you do? When loved ones are at stake, it is not as easy as it sounds. Doing the right thing sometimes requires courage and suffering for what is right.

My mom was famous for saying, "Being an adult means doing the right thing."

It is not always easy.

Many years later, I wonder what would have happened if I had taken just fifteen minutes and talked to my parents. Maybe all this suffering could have been avoided. I would have to live with that thought for the rest of my life. Best wishes, and hopefully you will do a better job than I did.

A current photo of me

God Bless us All!

Bryant Smith
21062 Redwood Lane
Mission Viejo, CA 92691-6622
(949) 583-2725
HeavensPlace@live.com